MW00616494

Absolutely phenomenal! Each chapter of *The Substance of a Woman* is so very captivating! Elaine Walker's passion and love for God are evident in this book. The way that she opens up the lives of these heroic women of the Bible is very intriguing. As you read through the pages, you will begin to see God's unconditional love for His daughters and how precious they are in His sight.

In *The Substance of a Woman*, Elaine beautifully describes how walking in God's will and obeying His commands can not only make a significant impact in our churches, families, and communities, but also have a great influence and contribute to positive change worldwide! What a blessing! By allowing us to take an intimate peek into her personal life and see the miracles that our Heavenly Father has performed for her, Elaine increases our faith and gives us courage to press on in life's challenges and difficulties, knowing that God is with us, too!

With every turn of each page, I was reminded not only to forgive myself of my past mistakes, but to love myself as God loves me! One very important fact that stands out among the many in *The Substance of a Woman* is that God did not create women by accident but on PURPOSE and for His PURPOSE!

Olivia McPhearson
Deaconess, Bible Way Christian Center, San Jose, California

The Substance of a Woman challenges you to foster personal growth and apply discipleship skills and leadership to all areas of your life. Elaine Walker brings her insight and wise counsel from God's Word to clear obstacles that are in your path. Elaine has served as a keynote speaker of several women's conferences and church events. Additionally, she has sponsored the San Jose New Restoration Baptist Church

Women's Conference for several years, where she calls God's Queens together to heal the broken, preach deliverance to the those who are bound, and set free those who are bruised.

The Substance of a Woman is not a should read. It is a must read.

Elder Charlie R. Reed, Jr.
Pastor, Higher Dimensions Church, Templeton, California

The Substance of a Woman is inspiring and insightful! Elaine Walker enlightens us about the intentionality of God, painting the picture so clearly and concisely that we as women really come to understand the substance we were created from. You will know another facet of our God and grow even more intimate with Him. You should encourage all women, especially young women, to read this book because it fosters self-worth and self-esteem.

Elaine literally brings the women of the Bible and their stories to life. The application she makes between the lives of these biblical personalities and women of today is simply outstanding! I want to go back and read their stories again with fresh eyes and a new perspective!

Rev. Lori Fairley Green
Assistant Pastor, Praises of Zion Church, Clearlake, California

The Substance of a Woman will take you on an exploration into the mind of God. Elaine Walker was able to extract indispensable insight from the Holy Spirit and illuminate the importance and contributions women have made to the Kingdom of God. With surgical precision, she removes the societal limitations and inadequacies that have shrouded women, and she methodically builds a platform that empowers women to stand in the fullness of God's glory. *The Substance of a Woman* will explain why God used a rib from Adam in the creative process of Eve. It also reveals the harmonization and cohesion that exist between husband and wife, man and woman, and God's never-ending love.

I strongly recommend reading *The Substance of a Woman*.

Rev. Dr. Shawn Curry
Agape Missionary Baptist Church, Tracy, California

Elaine Walker's *The Substance of a Woman* brings voice and value to the women of the Bible, some of whom are named, and even those who are named just by their circumstances. From Eve to the Woman at the Well, you will see God's love for all women and discover how we were created to bring substance to man, and therefore, to all of humanity. I pray that as every woman reads this book, they will see that God has a unique plan and purpose for each of their lives. I also pray that they will be encouraged to draw closer to God, and by doing so, will be able to walk out their God-given destiny.

Andrea Simmonds-Kwakye
Certified Professional Coach, San Jose, California

The Substance of a Woman is an incredible book packed with the life changing testimony of God Almighty. It is such a dense and comprehensive read it almost feels like it should be two books. It is full of hope and a great demonstration of God's safety net for all who will put their trust in Him. It is also encouraging to see the transparency of the author. Too often, pastor wives are reluctant to tell how they got to the other side of life's highs and lows. Elaine Walker is anything but reluctant. She shares her heart for God and her love for all women.

Vickie Wilson
Women's ministry leader and teacher and pastor's wife
for over 30 years, Gilroy, California

The Substance of a Woman

Discovering your value to God and your destiny in Him

ELAINE WALKER

The Substance of a Woman

by Elaine Walker

© 2021 by Elaine Walker. All rights reserved.

Editing by Adam Colwell's WriteWorks, LLC, Adam Colwell and Ginger Colwell

Cover and logo design by Myisha Jones
Typesetting by Katherine Lloyd, The DESK
Published by Adam Colwell's WriteWorks, LLC

Printed in the United States of America

Hardcover ISBN: 978-1-7371711-6-4
Softcover ISBN: 978-1-7371711-7-1
eBook ISBN: 978-1-7371711-8-8

All Scripture quotations, unless otherwise marked, are taken from the KING JAMES VERSION, public domain. Other Bible versions used are:

Scripture quotations marked (NASB) are taken from the NEW AMERICAN STANDARD BIBLE®, copyright© 1960, 1962, 1963, 1968, 1971, 1972, 1973, 1975, 1977, 1995 by The Lockman Foundation. Used by permission.

Scripture quotations marked (AMP) are taken from the AMPLIFIED® BIBLE, Copyright © 1954, 1958, 1962, 1964, 1965, 1987 by The Lockman Foundation. Used by Permission.

Scripture quotations marked (NIV) are taken from THE HOLY BIBLE, NEW INTERNATIONAL VERSION®. Copyright© 1973, 1978, 1984, 2011 by Biblica, Inc.™. Used by permission of Zondervan.

Scripture quotations marked (ESV) are taken from the THE HOLY BIBLE, ENGLISH STANDARD VERSION® Copyright© 2001 by Crossway, a publishing ministry of Good News Publishers. Used by permission.

Scripture quotations marked (MSG) are taken from the THE MESSAGE: THE BIBLE IN CONTEMPORARY ENGLISH, copyright©1993, 1994, 1995, 1996, 2000, 2001, 2002. Used by permission of NavPress Publishing Group.

Scripture quotations marked (NLT) are taken from THE HOLY BIBLE, NEW LIVING TRANSLATION, Copyright© 1996, 2004, 2007 by Tyndale House Foundation. Used by permission of Tyndale House Publishers, Inc., Carol Stream, Illinois 60188. All rights re-served. Used by permission.

While the author has made every effort to provide accurate internet addresses at the time of publication, neither the publisher nor the author assumes any responsibility for errors or for changes that occur after publication. Further, the publisher does not have any control over and does not assume any responsibility for author or third-party websites or their content.

Dedication

To my one and only true love, Derek LaMoin Walker.

When God whispered in my ear to write a book several years ago, I told you and you said, "If God told you to write it, then write the book." I had no clue how to write a book or where to start, but you had the most confidence in God—and in me. When I finally started writing the book, you encouraged me all along the way. When I wanted to give up, you reminded me that I could do all things through Christ Jesus who strengthens me. You were my biggest supporter, my number one fan, my love, and my king here on Earth. You were a living example of Ephesians 5:25: "Husbands, love your wives, even as Christ also loved the church, and gave himself for it." You gave your all to our family and to the Body of Christ, and this book is a testament of your love for me.

Now that the book is completed, I know I could never have written it without you. It was your love for me that inspired and led me to believe how special I was to God and to you. You loved me unconditionally and with such tenderness. Because of you, I know my worth is far above rubies.

I thank God every day for having a husband like you for 31 years. You were handpicked by God, and I will never forget you. Until we meet again.

To my Lord and Savior, Jesus Christ.

There are no words to express my deepest gratitude and honor to have written this book on your behalf. I cannot dedicate this book to you because it does not belong to me. I was just a vessel used by you to do your will. The pen cannot dedicate what is written by the author. You inspired me from the first page to the last. I can honestly say thank you for the privilege to speak to your daughters and soon to be daughters regarding the love you have for every one of them.

Thank you for loving me so much that I could write this book and confirm that your love is truly real and everlasting.

Contents

PART ONE
Who We Are in God

PART TWO:
How Important We Are to God

Acknowledgements

I would like to thank every woman I have encountered over my 35 years in ministry. I especially would like to say thank you to the women's Bible study group that meets with me every first Saturday of the month. You have encouraged me and given me a platform to share the Word of God with you, and I love the dedication and inspiration that you share with each other to encourage one another. You were my inspiration for every Bible study and every woman mentioned in this book. I love you all very much.

To my editor, Adam Colwell. I had no idea how to write a book, but if God said to do it, He said He would supply the resource to get it done, and that was you. You are an amazing man of God, and you are a gift to the body of Christ. I am so grateful to God for sending me an editor who truly loves the Lord. Thank you for standing with me through all of the trials and tribulations that I had to endure while writing this book. Even through my husband's death, you patiently waited for me to heal. We finally did it! You were exactly what I needed to carry out this commission.

To my daughter, Leah Walker. What would I do without you? You are my cheerleader and my best friend. You make me feel as though I can do anything. Thank you for your patience, love, and support. When I was so caught up in my other life obligations, you were there for me in so many ways. When I would forget, you were there to remind me. You carried out the tasks I did not have time to do, so I could continue to write. You were my listening ear, and when I asked for your opinion, you told me the truth and let me see another perspective. I love your love for God and your love for me. I love you.

To Myisha Jones. We have been working together in ministry for over 30 years, and I have seen you flourish on so many levels. I know that you are the one God has assigned in my life to hold my arms up as I submit to God's call. Thank you for always being there for me, especially when I asked you to design the book cover. I knew you could put into print what I had in my heart, and you did that! You are a jewel to me and the entire body of Christ.

To Shawn Finklea. You do not know this, but during a time when I did not think I could finish the book and Derek was so sick, you called me to ask about the book and how could you help me. I know that was God reminding me that even through my adversities, He was still there, and He used you to get me going once again. Thank you for being obedient to God and helping me when I truly needed it.

To Patrice Duncan. Writing a book takes a lot of time and attention, and while I was focusing on writing the book and taking care of my sick husband, you held down the preschool. I just want to publicly say thank you for all of your hard work and dedication.

To all of the church mothers who poured into me with wisdom and love, I thank you. Mother Mobley, Mother Catchings, Mother Hooks, Mother Prothro, Mother White, Mother Murphy, Mother Haylett, Mother McBride, Mother Delphine, and my grandmother, Mae Della Reed. All of you have been a great influence on the woman I have become today.

To New Restoration Church. You are my church family, and I am so glad to be a part of this great church. You have been there for me and encouraged me to be and do more for God. You will always have a special place in my heart.

Last but not least, my mother, Vernell Jones, who raised me to know the Lord and to be a strong, God-fearing woman. You were the one who loved me and taught me how beautiful and important I am to God. I love you.

Foreword

Vanderler L. Ellis
Ministry Development Leader
Pilgrim Church, Castro Valley, California

Elaine Walker and I first met in the early 1990's when her husband, Derek, invited my husband, Larry, and I over for dinner one Friday evening. When we arrived, Derek opened the door, grinning from ear to ear. He was so excited to have Pastor Ellis at his home. He introduced us to his wife, Elaine, who was setting the table, and I noticed how strategically she arranged each piece of dinnerware and how carefully she examined the way everything looked.

After reading *The Substance of a Woman*, I now understand why this task was so important: it was directly related to Sister Vernell's (Elaine's mother's) teaching during Elaine's formative years. Elaine walked over and greeted us with a warm, beautiful smile, welcoming us to her home.

Since that day, we have shared numerous meals with the Walker family. Derek, who was a master chef, often invited us to celebrate Thanksgiving Day dinners, New Year's Day gumbo, Raider game day barbeques, or any day that he felt like cooking a large meal to share with family and friends. Elaine was always right there as the perfect hostess, making sure that her guests were comfortable and enjoying themselves.

My first impression of Elaine was that she was a meek, kind, and gentle woman—and she is. I knew that Elaine was a Christian who was raised by godly parents and loved the Lord. What I did not know was how powerful, anointed, and gifted she was until I attended one of her women's conferences. During the conference, immediately following the welcome, the praise and worship began. Elaine started singing, shouting, and praising God with a loud, boisterous voice filled with passion and enthusiasm. It was so contagious, I could not contain myself and felt compelled to join in, which is saying a lot. Back then, I was quiet and reserved.

As Elaine shared the Word of God, I could feel the conviction of her heart. Elaine expressed sincere and genuine compassion for the women in the conference. She wanted us to know that no matter who we were or what our experiences had been, God loves us. Her words of encouragement reminded us as women that we are valuable to God. Anyone who engages Elaine in a conversation about the Lord will instantly be captivated by her deep love and gratitude for Him. She may even break out in praise!

I have read several books on women in the Bible. This is by far my favorite. Elaine's carefully written details of each biblical woman's story help the reader become aware of how much women have in common both then and now. *The Substance of a Woman* is relevant to the many issues we as women unfortunately still face today. It covers racial, gender, religious, and cultural concerns. Elaine has creatively captured the stories of both Old and New Testament women along with weaving in her own personal stories. When Christian women are transparent, the Holy Spirit has the ability to move in the hearts of all women. Personal stories are what connects us with the human spirit. Hopefully, Elaine's sharing of her lived experiences will inspire other women to let their guard down. Elaine is candid about who she was and is becoming. Her life and our lives parallel the lives of many women in the Bible. God has designed it that way.

In Part I: Who We Are in God, Elaine discusses the many roles and responsibilities that we hold as women. We are wives, mothers, cooks, teachers, nurses, and counselors, just to name a few. What is most important is our understanding that we are purposely and strategically created by God—and as women, we are to be forward thinking and forward progressing like Deborah, who was Israel's female judge and leader.

In Part II: How Important We Are to God, Elaine focuses on our significance as women. For instance, Anna, a widow and prophetess, was called by God to pray and fast for the people of the Lord. She ministered as a leader in the temple. She was 84 years old, proving that the age of a woman does not matter, but only her obedience and unwavering commitment to serve the Lord.

In Part III: How Important We Are to God's Purposes, Elaine affirms and encourages all women to pursue Kingdom purposes because of our spiritual gifting and to not allow our status, whether married or single, to hinder us. As married women, we have the opportunity to pour into the lives of our entire family. Supporting our husbands and raising children in the fear and admonition of the Lord is indeed fully operating in your Kingdom purpose. At the same time, Elaine shares that women who are single and love the Lord are in the best position to give glory to God because their time and hearts are not as divided as those who have husbands and children to care for. Single women with children have the responsibility to live by example what it means to love and honor God. This was demonstrated in the life of Eunice: as a single mother, she raised Timothy, who would become a young pastor and leader.

Finally, the book closes in Part IV: Let Your Substance Grow. In it, Elaine shares that in order for our substance to grow, every woman must cultivate her relationship with the Lord Jesus. We need to commune with God daily through the Holy Spirit. We must have a thirst for God that can only be quenched by the Lord Jesus. The Woman at the Well in John 4 did not understand she was missing a spiritual relationship, but Jesus knew exactly what she needed. Her encounter with Jesus changed her life forever. May we, as women, offer our mind, body, and spirit to the Lord Jesus so that He will fill us completely.

My prayer is that, through the Word of God and the wisdom Elaine shares in this book, the lives of many women across this country will be profusely impacted. Oh, the possibilities of changed lives for Jesus Christ! *The Substance of a Woman* is a call—an appeal for women of God in particular to face who we really are internally and to be real about our pain, our struggles, the emptiness we feel, and the burdens we carry. When we are honest with God, ourselves, and others, healing and restoration can begin. Then, by God's grace, we can disciple our sisters, especially those who have not surrendered their lives to Jesus Christ.

I believe that the Lord placed this book in Elaine's spirit for such a time as this. Don't let *The Substance of a Woman* pass you by. It will change your life.

Chapter 1

"And Adam said, This is now bone of my bones,
and flesh of my flesh: she shall be called Woman,
because she was taken out of Man."
(Genesis 2:23)

It is one of the most familiar yet inventive stories written in human history. Its visionary prose, not to mention its author, has inspired people young and old for generations.

Yet even after reading it time and again for as long as I can remember, I wasn't satisfied. Not at all.

I knew more was going on with the story than met the eye—and one particular question kept troubling me, demanding an answer. So, I decided to go straight to the source.

"God?" I asked. "Why the rib?"

His response changed my life—and I believe it'll do the same for you.

When I read the Bible, I almost always approach it with a sense of expectation. It never fails to show me something new or provide the direction I need for whatever I'm facing at that moment. But when I chose to study the first three chapters of Genesis, I wasn't as anticipatory as I thought I'd be. I mean, I already knew the story. God created the world and all that was in it, and then He formed Adam from the dust of the ground. When He decided it was not good for Adam to be alone, He made Eve. That's wonderful and all, but the intrigue doesn't happen until the serpent shows up. That's when the plot really takes off, right?

Wrong.

It's what Scripture teaches *before* sin is even introduced into the world that means so much to me as a woman.

We are many things to many people. We are daughters and confidants. We are girlfriends, wives, and lovers. We are mothers, maids, and cooks. We are doctors and nurses, teachers and counselors, hairstylists and clothes buyers, interior decorators and fashion experts. We are even taxi drivers for our children—all often in the same day and many times to the same people. We serve multiple and vital roles and are vested with remarkable responsibility and authority through all of these roles. We are nothing short of amazing, and even as little girls we seem to instinctively know this. The reason we play dress-up games and primp ourselves in the mirror with our toy makeup is because we innately understand that we are unique and deserving of special focus and attention.

We are to be looked upon. We are to be seen.

We are to be valued.

Yet many of us as women have so little self-esteem and so little sense of worth and purpose. We are incredibly adequate yet feel utterly inadequate. We are powerfully beautiful yet see ourselves as anything but attractive, perhaps even ugly. We are created by God as His masterpieces yet believe that the canvas of our lives is torn, our reflection in the gilded mirror irreparably broken.

> *We are to be looked upon. We are to be seen. We are to be valued.*

Why is this? First, there's no doubt that **negative or detrimental circumstances** play a persistent role in affecting how women perceive themselves. Issues pertaining to sexual, emotional, and physical abuse affect us, and having neglectful parents or coming from a broken home where one or both parents are gone can be undeniably impactful as well.

One young lady told me that she always felt something was wrong with her. She believed she was the reason that her mother stayed intoxicated and that her father abandoned them when she was an infant. She saw herself as being nothing more than a burden to her mother and, by extension, to everyone else around her.

Another cause for a woman's low self-esteem is **negative or zero affirmation from fathers or husbands**. Daughters look to their fathers, and wives to their husbands, for declarations of their worth and value in the same way that we as children of the King look for affirmation from God the Father. My father, Lee Jones, was steadfast and immovable when it came to God and our family's faith. He instilled within me and my five brothers the certainty that the Lord would always be there for us. My father was a provider. He was a visionary who successfully built a house in a more affluent area of San Jose, California in the mid-1970s when he was told he couldn't do it there because he was an African American. His faith was honored by God in that we never experienced an act of vandalism or violence as a result. He was also a pastor, and I loved going to church with him and helping him with whatever he needed for the congregation. My father was a great man, a mountain of stability and faith who I placed on a pedestal as his only daughter and the youngest of all of my siblings.

Yet he was a soft-spoken man. He didn't talk a lot, and he didn't speak words of affirmation to me like my mother, Vernell. With my father, you knew and did what was expected of you, and if you got out of line, he'd surely let you know. That's why I'll always remember the day when, at age eight, he told me, "You're getting fat. You need to lose some weight." I don't believe he intended to hurt me. But his words *stuck* and distorted all of the hundreds of positive things my mother told me—that I should dress for my body shape, wear nice clothes, and take care of my hair so I didn't present myself as frumpy, and that I should not try to fit with the images of women being portrayed on TV and in magazines. "You're fabulous!" she'd say, no matter my weight. "You're beautiful!" Yet somehow all of her positive words were dulled by my father's negative proclamation.

Another reason women perceive themselves wrongly is **ignorance fostered by both secular and some church cultures**. My mother always told me that I could do and be anything I wanted. She said I was strong and encouraged me to be self-sufficient. When I was getting ready to start kindergarten, she said to me, "Everybody isn't going to treat you like we treat you at home, so don't expect that when you start school." She wanted me to know that my self-esteem needed to come from within and not from what others said, did, or expected of me. I didn't know it as a little child, but this was radical thinking even for the late 1960s. Male roles were still more prominently seen than women's were. The women's lib movement was only beginning to emerge. Girls and women were still seen to be subservient in the secular culture.

Sadly, that was, and still remains, the case in most church cultures. Some churches are now more accepting of women in leadership and authority, but many still support the idea that women are *only* to fulfill their vital roles of raising the family and caring for the home. They are not to preach and not to teach. Back then, they were to act and dress a certain way in church, prim and proper with long dresses to the ankle, while at the same time the secular culture was telling them to be radical and unafraid to don a miniskirt and show some cleavage.

Women are essential to God's purposes for the Earth

Even worse, though, is that the Bible was, and often still is, *misappropriated* to encourage the erroneous perception within these two male-dominated cultures that women are secondary. That we are weak. That we

4

are the problem. That we are not strong. In truth, the pages of Scripture are filled with accounts of powerful women of God who rocked the worldly and religious cultures of their day—and the Bible teaches that women are essential to God's purposes for the Earth, valued by Him, indispensable to men, and an all-important and mandatory part of our homes as well as both the secular and church culture.

What God showed me from the Adam and Eve story in Genesis, and in what He told me in response to my frustrated "Why the rib?" query, didn't just demolish all of these perceptions—it annihilated them. As He revealed the truths I'm going to unfold for you in this book, I feverishly wrote them down and fashioned my notes into a teaching that I first presented as a guest speaker at a service dedicated to women at Macedonia Baptist Church in Menlo Park, California. As I went forward to begin my message, I perceived that I had something noteworthy to share. I knew it was from God, and I felt it was going to be good.

But I had no idea what was going to happen.

Women came forward and gave their lives to the Lord. Others who were lifelong Christians recommitted themselves to Him. I was blown away! Afterward, several women came up to me and hugged my neck as they wiped away the tears that smudged their mascara into streaks of joyful surrender. "It was so empowering!" "I *am* important to God!" "I *do* have value in His Kingdom purposes!" In my spirit, I saw broken chains piled at their feet. Like the little girl in pigtails sprinting to her daddy and jumping into his arms, these precious daughters of the King had run into their Heavenly Father's arms, leaped into His embrace, and soaked in the worth He felt for them and the destiny He had for them.

Are you ready to do that—and to discover your substance as

a woman given especially to you by God Himself? Then kick off your heels, pour yourself a cup of chamomile tea or a caramel macchiato, and plunge into your chaise lounge. Then, if you'd like, open up your Bible to Genesis chapter 1. It won't be hard to find—because it all starts at the very beginning.

PART ONE

Who We Are in God

Chapter 2

"And God said, Let us make man in our image,
after our likeness: and let them have dominion over the fish
of the sea, and over the fowl of the air, and over the cattle,
and over all the earth, and over every creeping thing that
creepeth upon the earth. So God created man in his own
image, in the image of God created he him;
male and female created he them."
(Genesis 1:26-27)

Can you identify the one word in this passage of Scripture that I believe is one of the most overlooked words in all the Bible? Do you see it?

Them.

God "let *them* have dominion…male and female created he *them*."

From the very start, the Lord **purposefully and strategically** created women. We did not come about accidentally or as an after-thought. God had women on His mind before the actual creation of Adam. Notice the chronological progression of God's creative process. First, He created everything humanity needed: day and night, the water and the sky, the land and the seas, the plants and trees with their fruit and seeds, and the sun and the moon with the stars. Everything was perfect and complete. Then, in Genesis 2, the Lord unfolds more of His plan.

"And the Lord God formed man of the dust of the ground,
and breathed into his nostrils the breath of life; and man

became a living soul...And the Lord God said, It is not good that the man should be alone; I will make him an help meet for him. And out of the ground the Lord God formed every beast of the field, and every fowl of the air; and brought them unto Adam to see what he would call them: and whatsoever Adam called every living creature, that was the name thereof. And Adam gave names to all cattle, and to the fowl of the air, and to every beast of the field; but for Adam there was not found an help meet for him." (Genesis 2:7, 18-20)

Look at God's **thoughtfulness** in the way He created women. He recognized that Adam was lonely and decided He needed to bring Eve on the scene. Notice, however, that it was Adam who had to learn how to care for and name the animals *before* God created Eve. This, therefore, trained Adam how to later name Eve. It also gave him a vital job—to be a provider, to be the head, and to be able to protect the woman. God created Adam (men) and "put him into the garden of Eden to dress it and to keep it" (Genesis 2:15), to husband and care for the gift He provided—then God created Eve (women) once Adam was prepared to husband and care for *her*. This progression was intentional. One act of creation prepared for the next.

In addition, both men and women were formed in the likeness of God to have **divine purpose to represent Him** here on Earth. There was no gender better than the other in the Lord's creation; both equally expressed His likeness together. The word "image" in the Hebrew means "a shade, a resemblance." When we think of a shadow, we picture a man and woman standing next to each other, the sun at their backs, and their shadows apart, distinct from one another. But that's not how God created them in relation to His image. Instead, the two shadows merge to form one shadow that displays the likeness of God; it is *only* by the merged shadow that we can see the true, complete image of the Lord.

Moreover, God's character qualities—love, intellect, free will—are equivalently displayed through men and women together. His divine purpose as His earthly representatives, to be fruitful and productive to His glory, is achieved in the same quantity, quality, and degree through men and women together. The very fruit of the Spirit from Galatians 5:22-23 of love, joy, peace, longsuffering, gentleness, goodness, faith, meekness, and temperance are accomplished through *men and women together*—not just in marital relationships, but in any relational interaction between men and women. Thus, the equality and value of women with men are permanently struck on the record of time in Genesis 1:26-27, positioning both to carry out His plan as a coequal duo who cannot fully achieve His purposes apart from one another.

Mary was a young lady of remarkable strength and fortitude.

This truth is wonderfully displayed in the way God used Mary and Joseph as the earthly parents of Jesus Christ. Mary was a young lady of remarkable strength and fortitude. She was likely no more than 15 years of age when the angel Gabriel appeared to her as recorded in Luke 1:26-38. By then, she was betrothed to Joseph, meaning she was engaged to be married to him, and she was a virgin awaiting sexual relations with him until after they were wed. All was proper for their relationship and the culture.

Then the angel spoke. "Hail, thou that art highly favoured, the Lord is with thee: blessed art thou among women ... Fear not, Mary: for thou hast found favour with God. And, behold, thou shalt conceive in thy womb, and bring forth a son, and shalt call his name Jesus. He shall be great and shall be called the Son of the Highest: and the Lord God shall give unto him the throne of his father David: And he shall reign over the house of Jacob for ever; and of his kingdom there shall be no end."

I can imagine her fingers touching her parted lips. She could hardly believe what she heard, much less what she was seeing. *This is an angel of the Lord?* she wondered. *I'm going to give birth to the One to be given the throne forever?*

"How shall this be," she asked haltingly, "seeing I know not a man?"

"The Holy Ghost shall come upon thee, and the power of the Highest shall overshadow thee," Gabriel responded. "Therefore also that holy thing which shall be born of thee shall be called the Son of God." He also shared that her cousin Elizabeth, who was barren, was also going to have a child. "For with God nothing shall be impossible."

Heart pounding, a smile came to her face. *Oh, God, can it be? Your Son? The Messiah?* Pride mixed with holy fear welled within her heart. "Behold the handmaid of the Lord; be it unto me according to thy word." We can tell by Mary's response, as she complied to give herself for the use of the Lord's plan, that she had a heart for God.

CHOSEN BY GOD: MARY

Mary was chosen by God because she had a relationship with Him. According to Jewish custom, it was the parents' responsibility to teach their children from generation to generation about God's provision. Mary believed their report. The angel said she was highly favored by God, and that was why He chose her, a peasant girl from Nazareth—a place that, in biblical times, was looked upon as a ghetto. People there were viewed as impoverished and uneducated. The city had no economic value, so anyone who came from Nazareth was marginalized because it was a poor, non-thriving town. No wonder Nathaniel, one of Jesus' disciples, later asked,

"Can any good thing come out of Nazareth?" (John 1:46, NASB) Also notice that even in her praise to God, Mary mentions, later in Luke 1, how God chose her over all other women. She worships God for exalting her from a low estate so that those who thought themselves to be better would have to look up to her. God validated her worth and Mary's esteem was elevated.

When God uses you to do His will, a great sense of value and a feeling of importance overwhelm you, and feelings of goodness, joy, and fulfillment overtake you. This is a wonderful illustration of God's love towards those who are less fortunate and of His validation of them to be used by Him. To God, it does not matter where you come from, what your economic status is, or what your level of education or your pedigree is: God will use anyone that has a willing heart and a love for Him. Sometimes we as women have feelings of inadequacy or a low self image, but you are made with a substance that makes you victorious so you can declare from His Word, "I can do all things through Christ who strengthens me." (Philippians 4:13) God will place inside of you the desire and passion to carry out His will. Mary had purpose, and her passion was for God. God presented her purpose through the angel Gabriel, and she began to live in her purpose.

It is when we have a relationship with God that we can carry out the purpose that God has for our lives. As we draw closer to the Lord through prayer, worship, studying God's Word, fellowship, and ministry, God's plan for our lives becomes clearer. Every woman of God has a purpose and a destiny. We must be steadfast and immovable in our faith in God. We must foster a love relationship with the creator of our soul. We cannot be ready to do God's will today and then change our mind tomorrow. No matter what the obstacles we face in life (and we will face many), He is still the God who controls the universe and loves His daughters. He is still the one who created us to be strong and to be a help.

As we look at the obstacles, struggles, and adversity Mary was about to endure, we will see her amazing strength and trust in her God. As women, we face many different trials—finances, single motherhood, jobs, education, marriage, medical issues, and even the stress of trying to keep it all together. But let's be like Mary and conquer them all through faith and perseverance.

After the angel departed, Mary allowed everything that had just happened to sink in. She realized, according to the Jewish law, that she could be stoned to death for being pregnant outside of marriage. She'd surely be shunned by her family, her friends— everyone. But she knew what the angel had said, and her love for God and her faith in the Lord strengthened her resolve and swept away her fears. She also thought of her husband-to-be. *I'm going to go to this man, tell him that I'm pregnant, and say that God Himself put the child in my womb? How can he possibly believe me?* Then she recalled that the angel had said her cousin was also miraculously pregnant. *I will go visit Elizabeth. I know she'll be a comfort because she'll believe me and celebrate with me.*

MARY'S ELDER CONFIDANT

Mary was the perfect example of who women are in God. The first obstacle she had to face was being pregnant before the marriage. *No one* would believe that she conceived a child by the Holy Ghost. Then there was the issue of telling Joseph and whether or not he would believe her. How could it be that she was given this wonderful news and at the same time she was faced with death and abandonment? Of course, these things happen in our lives as well. There are days of jubilation and then there are days of weeping and sorrow, but as David said, "weeping may endure for a night, but joy cometh in the morning." (Psalm 30:5)

Mary's morning came during her three month stay with Elizabeth. What happened when these two women of God came together? Worship! God's Spirit was manifest in their presence. "For where two or three are gathered together in my name, there am I in the midst of them." (Matthew 18:20) God came down and rearranged the whole situation. Heavenly accommodations superseded earthly situations. Can you imagine being in the room with Mary and Elizabeth as the power of the Lord moved through them? Shekinah Glory! The glory of the Lord was in the room with them, and they began to lift each other up in praise. When women come together in one accord, they can turn any situation around! I truly believe Satan knows how powerful we are together, and that is why he does his best to keep us apart or make us envious toward one another.

It is so important to have another woman, a sister in the Lord, to be your elder confidant and praise partner when God asks you to do the incredible and experience His divine purpose for your life. It will only enhance who you are in God when you have someone to walk this journey with you who is strong in faith and full of wisdom. She will rejoice with you, encourage you in the Lord, be with you through your dark nights, and celebrate your morning times. She will tell the truth in love when you're wrong and praise you when you're right. Who is that person for you? Seek out your elders for guidance and wisdom, for this will empower you and encourage you to keep moving forward.

Imagine how rich that time must've been for Mary as Elizabeth ministered to her to let her know everything was going to be alright, that God was indeed with her, and that she had more than enough strength to return to Joseph and tell him everything the angel had shared with her. As Titus 2:4 declares, God has created older women to "teach the young women to be sober, to love their husbands, to love their children."

By the time Mary left Elizabeth, she had received complete provision and preparation from the Lord. God supplied exactly what Mary needed during this time in her life, and God will always do the same for us. There is an answer for every problem. We need to keep our faith and trust in the Lord, no matter the situation. We also need to stay in constant prayer, which keeps us in constant communication with God. We must praise Him and worship Him through the circumstance, which will maintain intimacy between us and God. There are going to be times when we face adversity, but God created us to be victorious in every situation. Mary was ready for the challenges to come, beginning with telling her fiancé that she was pregnant by the Holy Ghost—something that had never happened before, was utterly impossible apart from God. She did not know how God was going to help Joseph understand or believe her. Such courage was unprecedented, yet Mary trusted the Lord as she approached Joseph. I picture him busy in his carpenter shop.

"Mary, my beloved. Welcome back!" He went to embrace her, but then saw her midsection. By now, she was beginning to show. His eyes widened. "What is this?"

Mary told him everything the angel had said, her voice bold and unwavering. *God, it's all up to you now.*

I imagine Joseph threw down his hammer. He paced back and forth. It was obvious he was upset. Any man's natural reaction would be to feel betrayed, conclude that she was unfaithful, was obviously no longer a virgin, and was therefore not worthy enough for them to complete the marriage. But Scripture says there was a difference with Joseph: he was a righteous man. He still wanted to protect Mary.

> *We can live in confidence that He will come through.*

After thinking over what Mary had said, I can see Joseph walking over and taking her hand. "I care for you," he told her. "I don't want anything to happen to you. I will divorce you quietly so that no one will know." During biblical times, Jewish custom dictated that being engaged was like being married. The only difference was the couple did not live together nor did they engage in sexual relations. Papers of divorce had to be acquired to annul an engagement. "I won't expose you. I love you, Mary," Joseph pleaded, "but I just can't—well, I don't know what to believe." I envision him then looking down at the ground, and Mary followed his gaze to a rugged piece of wood and the rusty nail protruding from its edge.

Mary likely returned to her room as dusk was settling in to prepare herself for bed. *God, I know what you told me. I know you are with me. I trust you now to see me through, no matter what happens next!* She found herself rubbing her belly, and while sleep wouldn't come, her prayers were ceaseless. Mary was confronting the one thing she suspected she'd have to face: her fiancé leaving her with no protection and no husband.

What else could she do but trust in God to deliver her? Faced with heartbreak, abandonment, ridicule, embarrassment, and possibly death, it was here when Mary could've easily given up and turned her back on God. She could have decided that all of this was not worth the trouble. *I said "yes" to the Lord, and now I am pregnant with no husband and no finances. I will be an outcast and my parents will disown me, all because I said "yes" to God.*

But Mary did not reject God. I'm sure she remembered the stories of Moses and the Red Sea, Daniel in the lion's den, Elijah on Mount Carmel, Deborah in battle, Esther saving her people from death, and God's provision for Ruth and Naomi. *If God did it for them, surely He will do it for me!* When we stand in our strength, in our faith, and in what we know about our God, we will see the salvation of the Lord! When we think about His goodness and all He has already done in our lives, we can live in confidence that He will come through.

Suddenly she heard footsteps approaching—coming quickly.

"Mary, you won't believe it!" Joseph said, and he laughed. It was joyous, just like the day she first met him. "I couldn't believe you at first," he continued, "but now it's happened to me—to us! An angel appeared to me in a dream. I now know! You were telling the truth, the incredible truth!" Mary watched Joseph fall to the ground on one knee. "I worship the Lord! I, too, accept His word. And Mary?" He looked right at her, his face positively beaming. "You *will* be my wife! I will love you for all of my days. Somehow, some way, we will be father and mother to God's Son. Jesus. I like the name, don't you? 'God saves!'"

God provided a way when it seemed there was no way out. Like David said, "I have been young, and now am old; yet have I not seen the righteous forsaken, nor his seed begging bread." (Psalm 37:25) God will not abandon you! Look to Him when you're not sure what to do and when the situation looks bleak. Stand still and know He is God! When you stand still, you are standing in faith. When you stand still, you are upright and unmoved by anything that tries to knock you off your course. If He did it before, He will do it again! Don't give up on the Lord. There will be times when you think God is not there or that He doesn't hear you. God is always there, and He hears your every prayer. When trouble has come my way, I have often repeated to myself, "God, I trust you for my life. You will come through. No weapon formed against me shall prosper." Sure enough, He has come to my rescue every time.

Mary surely wept tears of joy that Joseph accepted her and tears of adoration for God's power and grace! But her story of strength hardly ends there. Fast forward to the final weeks of her pregnancy. By now, she had endured all the pleasures and discomforts of pregnancy minus all the modern conveniences most of us take for granted today. Joseph received disturbing news: Caesar Augustus had issued a decree that a census was required. That meant each family had to journey to the hometown of the man's lineage—in this case, Bethlehem, for Joseph was a descendant of David. The journey from Nazareth to Bethlehem was no walk in the park, especially with Mary about to go into labor. The cities were about 70 miles apart, a three-day trek, and the path was rocky and dry. Imagine yourself in Mary's sandals. It was difficult to walk, let alone travel all that way with swollen feet, contractions, lower pelvic pain, and back pain. She was dusty, dirty, and tired.

Finally, they arrived in Bethlehem, and Mary's hopes rose when they first entered town. But they were quickly dashed when they arrived at the inn. "We have no rooms available," the innkeeper said. "You must go away!"

"What do you mean, 'No rooms?'" Mary said frantically. "Can't you see I'm about to have a child. *Make* one available!"

"It is impossible!" he said. "Everyone is here for the census. We can't properly house the people we have. But I have a stable. It's out back. Go there. It's all I can do." He shut the door.

Oh God! she thought. *I'm worn out. I'm filthy. I'm in pain. How can I be carrying the Savior of the world and there be no room for Him? Did I just imagine it all?* But Mary was the epitome of strength in action. She resolved to go into a barn to deliver God's only begotten Son. Mary carried on with trust in her God and the substance that He created within her. She gave birth to Jesus in a stable and made do with strips of cloths to wrap Him. Never once did she complain about the situation or the conditions she encountered—and God knew she was able to carry out His plan.

With God, there is purpose and a plan for every woman's life. What is your purpose? How are you carrying it out? How are you responding to the obstacles and the adversity? Are you standing in trust or fear? God does not give us the spirit of fear. As you pray to our Father, ask Him for guidance and wisdom on how to move through trials. Have a plan, talk it over with your elder, and keep progressing forward. Mary never stopped. In the days to come, shepherds visited, magi arrived with gifts, and many marveled at her baby son! Mary endured it all with a mix of joy and reverence. Then, right after the magi's visit, Joseph woke her up in the middle of the night, not because of a crying infant but something far worse.

"Mary," he said, "the angel of the Lord has again appeared to me in a dream. He told me, 'Get up, take the child and his mother, and escape to Egypt. Stay there until I tell you, for Herod is going to search for the child to kill him.'"

The king? Mary thought. *My Lord, why would the king want to murder Jesus, the promised Messiah? How can anyone escape a king's decree?* Fear rose in her heart—but so did something else, quenching its power. God! He had made a way of escape for her and her family. She didn't hesitate. They gathered their things and set off for a journey far longer than the one that had brought them from Nazareth. They traveled to Egypt and stayed until it was safe to return to their hometown.

What great strength Mary had, both physical and spiritual, to have gone through such adversity, only to be victorious through it all. Only a *woman of God* could survive this kind of trial and remain committed to the plan of her Lord. Throughout the pregnancy, there were feelings of disbelief and disappointment followed by great joy and outbursts of praise caused by God's miracles and provision. In it all, Mary remained constant in her faith in God, and He worked out everything because she refused to give up. Her mind was made up that she was going to carry out God's plan for her life *no matter what!*

God will do the same for you, His daughters, as you continue to be steadfast and immovable. Each trial strengthens you to get through the next. We must remember that what we encounter is part of God's master plan to fulfill His purpose. All that Mary went through prepared her to achieve God's will for her family and, ultimately, the entire world: salvation through the shed blood of His Son—rusty nails pounded into a rugged cross.

In the end, Mary's purpose was to bring Jesus into the world, something she was uniquely created to do as a woman. Joseph's purpose was to cover Mary and protect her, for in protecting her he was also protecting Jesus. Mary *nurtured*; Joseph *protected*. Their roles were different, but their purpose was the same, and their importance in accomplishing God's purpose was equal. The two were intertwined; they had to work together, in agreement and in mutual help and strength. It's when we obey the Lord—men in the roles He's given to them and women in the roles He's given to us—that God's purposes are fulfilled.

Mary and Joseph also *glorified* God through their roles. As women and men, our purpose is to lift up God in all that we do and in our praise of Him. We are created to bless and glorify the name of the Lord; indeed, if we do not, the very stones will cry out in praise! (Luke 19:40) Women and men are both wired and required to worship Him, and this worship is the same to God as long as it comes from a true heart. If it's coming out of a woman's heart, God receives it; it if comes from a man, God receives it. It is of equal worth and value to Him.

> *God created men and women to exert and share co-dominion.*

No wonder, then, that God created men and women to **exert and share *co-dominion*** with power and authority to fulfill the will of God on Earth. This means that whatever it is that God has ordained for you to do or purposed you to experience as a woman, you are to do it without reservation. You are created to reflect Him, and His reflection will emulate His holiness, strength, righteousness, goodness, truth, salvation—and even His healing power!

FIERCE DETERMINATION

When I first became pregnant with my daughter, Leah, my doctor discovered a tumor on my liver. It was growing at a rapid pace, so much so that the doctor I was referred to for treatment said there was no way my baby could develop properly with the tumor also growing within me. She said I would have to terminate the pregnancy.

I couldn't believe it. *How can I abort my child?* I thought.

"Is that my only option?" I asked.

"It's either you or the baby," she said firmly. "The tumor is going to outgrow the baby, and you're not going to survive if you carry this baby to term."

I was not about to make a decision at that moment. "Let me pray about it," I told her, and I left the hospital with my husband, Derek, and my mother, Vernell, despairing. We rode home in silence, but I knew where to turn.

Whenever I'm faced with a severe trial, I go inside the walk-in closet in my bedroom, close the door, and seek God's face for direction. I don't depart until I know I have received instruction from Him. I fervently pled with the Lord—not for my life, or even the life of my unborn child—but for *His will*. I knew that if I did what He said, I couldn't fail. Ultimately, I received my orders. "When I get up," I said to God, "the first thing I see when I open my Bible will be my answer."

I left the closet, found my King James Bible, and opened it. My eyes riveted on Luke 8:48.

"And he said unto her, Daughter, be of good comfort: thy faith hath made thee whole; go in peace."

That was it! There was no reservation. Derek and I went back to the doctor, and I told her, "Look, God said that I'm healed and to go in peace with my child."

Her mouth dropped open and her eyebrows arched. She stiffened in her chair. "You're crazy!" she declared. "If that's what you want, then I refuse to treat you!"

I grabbed my purse, got up, and walked out. *I don't want you to treat me,* I mused. *I know what God said!* The Lord then led me to a precious Indian doctor, Bina, who said she would not only treat me, but she would help me all the way through to the birth. She also referred me to a liver specialist, and over the next several months we watched as the tumor continued to grow—but so did the baby. By the start of my second trimester, the tumor was the size of an orange, but the child was outgrowing it! In fact, by the time I was ready to give birth, the baby was so big she had to be delivered by Caesarean section. She was almost 10 pounds.

Since I was going to be opened up anyway, the doctor decided to also do an exploratory surgery to check on the tumor. She said she rubbed her hand all over my liver—and the tumor was gone! Just two weeks earlier, it was there; the sonogram showed it as big as day. But, just as God promised, by the time Leah was born, *poof!* He had terminated the tumor! Today, Leah is happy and healthy as my one and only child, a reality of faith in my living God!

Once I got my direction from God, nothing was going to change my mind. That fierce determination exists in all women—but that's the difference between a woman of God and a woman who does not know the Lord. One will hear the voice of the Lord and act; the other will not. It's all about having a relationship with Jesus Christ. He will help you transcend what seems to be the logical or even right thing to do. When I was first told that I had to have an abortion, my mother was frightened by the doctor's prognosis. "Just do it," she told me later. "You can always have another child, but I can never have another Elaine." My mother was a Christian, but she was scared, and fear attacked her faith.

"I'm going to be fine," I reassured her after my prayer closet experience. "God said my faith has made me whole. I believe in Him!" I re-declared that to her time and again. Even godly people can give you advice that goes against what the Lord tells you, but as a woman of God, He will empower you to stand your ground. When I was young, my father always said, "If God tells me to walk through this wall, it is my responsibility to walk. It's God's responsibility to move the wall."

Yet perhaps the most remarkable aspect of that entire season of my life was how Derek supported me. When I told him what the Lord had told me, he was in immediate agreement with me. I'm sure he had the same fears as my mother, perhaps even more so. But he understood that God had created the two of us to be in *co-dominion,* equal partners to execute His purposes. Derek never wavered. He took care of me throughout days of seemingly endless illness when the tumor and pregnancy combined to bring perpetual pain and weight loss. In the end, we endured together in faith. Our mutual strength and trust in God brought us through to victory!

Finally, God was **artistically creative** in how He created women. Just look at us! We are beautiful, the loveliest of all of God's creations—and it's not just because of who created us, but because of where our creation *originated.* The Lord created Adam from the dust of the Earth. But He brought the woman forth from the rib bone of His prize creation. God then touched and formed, shaped, and sculpted, manifesting her from that unique origin.

All other creations on land were created from dust, but not woman! We are the only creation of Earth that is created from bone. Just like valuable resources such as oil, silver, and gold needs to be mined from the Earth, the Lord extracted from Adam the very essence of what makes up a woman. God hid things of great value inside the Earth—and He did the same within Adam. Not only are they of great value, but they enhance the lives of those who possess them. This means that we are a rare commodity, a masterpiece of great value, the crescendo of God's creative expression.

We enhance the lives of those we come in contact with and those who possess us as wives, daughters, mothers, and sisters. With women, God truly saved the best for last—and because of how He formed us, it's no accident that we are exquisitely beautiful to behold. Our physical loveliness and our inner attractiveness comes from the very beauty God created us with. The definition of beauty is telling. It is "a combination of qualities, such as shape, color, or form, that pleases the aesthetic senses, especially the sight." We are beauty personified because that's the way God made us.

> *With women, God truly saved the best for last.*

Now that you are getting a sense of how strong and beautiful you are and how gloriously and strategically you were created, I want you to stop right now and read this passage from Psalm 139 as though it is the first time you've ever seen it. I want you to speak these verses into your life and personalize them. Allow what they declare about you to be placed not only in your mindset, but to be embedded in your very soul—because whatever is in your soul cannot be taken away!

> "For You formed my inward parts;
> You wove me in my mother's womb.
> I will give thanks to You, for I am fearfully and wonder-
>   fully made;
> Wonderful are Your works,
> And my soul knows it very well.
> My frame was not hidden from You,

When I was made in secret,
And skillfully wrought in the depths of the earth;
Your eyes have seen my unformed substance;
And in Your book were all written
The days that were ordained for me,
When as yet there was not one of them.
How precious also are Your thoughts to me, O God!
How vast is the sum of them!"
(Psalm 139:13-17, NASB)

Glory to God, and get ready, because you're about to discover what God's creative process speaks to your *substance* that is truly remarkable. All of God's intentionality, thoughtfulness, and artistry culminated as He brought woman into glorious reality—and it all started with a deep sleep.

Chapter 3

"And the Lord God caused a deep sleep to fall upon
Adam, and he slept: and he took one of his ribs,
and closed up the flesh instead thereof; And the rib,
which the Lord God had taken from man,
made he a woman, and brought her unto the man."
(Genesis 2:21-22)

This passage reveals the first of the two substances that make up women—the bone. Bone is the strongest substance in the human body, and it makes up the body's form. In addition, bone enables us to move forward. Without bone, we'd be limp and unable to function.

But God doesn't just use any old bone from Adam to create Eve. He takes it from the rib cage on Adam's side. This is remarkably intentional and significant. The rib cage protects life. Some of our most vital organs are contained within the rib cage. When God chose a bone from the rib cage to use in the creation of women, He already had in mind what she would be able to do. She would be strong, protect life, and move herself and others forward. These are the characteristics that begin to make up the substance of a woman.

Is it any wonder that Adam, the one given authority by God to name everything He created, named her "Eve?" Eve means "giver of life." That was what Adam felt she was to him and to all of creation—a giver of life! He saw her as his *life enhancer*, one who could not only birth life, but enhance his life as well as the lives of others!

Do you see that? You need to *know* this as a woman, and place it into your soul. Even as you are going through your own trials today, you are a person who enhances life. You are made from the strongest substance in the human body. You are crafted and predestined by God to protect life and move yourself and others forward to their purposes in Him, to His glory!

WE ARE STRONG TO PROTECT LIFE: JOCHEBED

As women, God created us to be like a lioness, strong and poised to go above and beyond to protect her family. A phenomenal example of this kind of woman from the Bible is Moses' mother, Jochebed. Edith Deen, in her wonderful 1955 book, *All of the Women of the Bible*, said that we see in Jochebed some of the qualities of Mary, mother of Jesus, who recognized her baby as destined by God for His special purpose. "Like Mary, Jochebed must also have seen imitations of her child's high destiny and 'pondered them in her heart' (Luke 2:19). And Jochebed, again like Mary, was willing to suppress her own maternal love and to dedicate her son to that which he had been called by God."

At the time Jochebed gave birth to Moses, this remarkable woman knew that the Pharaoh had issued an edict to midwives to kill all male Hebrew children at birth. This was not unlike the order issued centuries later by King Herod that all male children in Bethlehem two years old and younger be murdered in his attempt to thwart the life of Jesus. Yet Jochebed managed to save her son from the Pharaoh's command during the first three months of his life. However, when she knew she could no longer risk keeping him hidden, Jochebed was undeniably brave in sending her child down the mighty Nile River in

> *As women, God created us to be like a lioness.*

28

a fragile basket made of reeds in a valiant, but risky, attempt to save her baby's life. Her faith in God to protect her baby from crocodiles, carnivorous lizards, and other creatures that might be lurking in the river's depths was nothing short of amazing.

I can see Jochebed praying to her God as she placed her infant son in the dangerous Nile. She had to consider, *Am I doing the right thing? Is God going to save my baby? Do I have the strength to do this?* Her only choices were either to place her baby in the river where he would possibly be saved or to hold on to her son and wait for Pharaoh's soldiers to arrive and kill him. What a struggle she must have experienced. Just like Mary, Jochebed had to resolve to trust in the God she served. I can see her saying, as she laid the little ark in the water, "The God of Abraham, Isaac, Jacob, and Joseph, go with my child." What faith this woman had in her God—and what wisdom God gave to her to send her daughter Miriam along to look after the baby as he passed through the river's marshy reeds.

Just look at how God made a way.

"And the daughter of Pharaoh came down to wash herself at the river; and her maidens walked along by the river's side; and when she saw the ark among the flags, she sent her maid to fetch it. And when she had opened it, she saw the child: and, behold, the babe wept. And she had compassion on him, and said, This is one of the Hebrews' children. Then said his sister to Pharaoh's daughter, Shall I go and call to thee a nurse of the Hebrew women, that she may nurse the child for thee? And Pharaoh's daughter said to her, Go. And the maid went and called the child's mother. And Pharaoh's daughter said unto her, Take this child away, and nurse it for me, and I will give thee thy wages. And the women took the child, and nursed it.

And the child grew, and she brought him unto Pharaoh's daughter, and he became her son. And she called his name Moses: and she said, Because I drew him out of the water." (Exodus 2:5-10)

Here comes God again! None other than the Pharaoh's own daughter found him. The baby ended up alive and well in the very palace of the one who was trying to kill him. Yet God didn't stop there! Not only did He save the child and place him in the courts of the Egyptian god-king, but Jochebed got paid to nurse her own son! Jochebed had complete trust in God for her son, and because of her unwavering faith, God gave her beyond what she had asked for.

We need to believe that God will do what is best for us. He loves us and cares about the things we care about, even when we're in situations that seem too much for us to bear. Through those difficult moments, God will sometimes lead us to make difficult decisions that we do not want to make. In these times, fear and doubt can get in the way and try to convince us that God will not see us through. That's when we are to remember that in times past God has never failed, and He won't start now. Our situation may look impossible, or even frightening like Jochebed's dilemma, but God has our life's destiny in His hands. "All things work for the good for those who love God and are called according to His purpose." (Romans 8:28) You have purpose. God has a plan. He'll step in and perform the miraculous.

Surely, Jochebed never thought she'd be able to nurse her baby again. But to be paid for it, too? That's the "exceedingly abundantly above all that we can ask or think" (Ephesians 3:20) kind of blessing God gives! He wants to perform these blessings in our lives every day, but we will not experience them if we do not trust Him. In the life of Jochebed, God used mother, sister, and even Pharaoh's daughter to save the baby's life—and all three women had a purpose to ensure that Moses would ultimately be used to deliver the nation of Israel out of harsh and bitter bondage.

All women, whether they are believers in God or non-believers, are made of the same substance and possess the same inner strength, but it's only the woman who knows the Lord who will go beyond the natural and move into the supernatural. The woman who has no relationship with the Creator can only use her natural strength in difficult situations, but Jochebed's situation shows that there are some circumstances that call for supernatural assistance to be victorious. In her case, two women knew the God of the universe; one (Pharaoh's daughter) did not. Yet God will use anyone to fulfill His plan in any way He needs. It may be something as great as being the mother of the deliverer, something as small as being the sister who chaperones the basket of the baby deliverer down the Nile, or something as significant as Pharaoh's daughter being strong enough to convince her father to allow her to raise a Hebrew child in the palace, not knowing he would be the child who would deliver the Israelites out of the bondage of her own Egyptian people. No matter what, God will use whomever He desires! He will always get the victory—and when He gets the victory, we get the victory.

My sister-in-law Angela was a devout woman of God. Her entire life was committed to God, and she loved Him with all of her heart. She had to raise her three children on her own because her husband became addicted to crack cocaine early in her marriage and left the family. She was a housewife, but she had to go back to work to provide for her children. How she paid the rent, put food on the table, clothed her children, and paid her tithes was a testament of how God provided for His own. She always said that God took care of her and her kids, and that she could always depend on Him to come through.

Angela had to overcome many adversities. She was evicted

from her home and had to find a new place to live. She was a single mom and sole provider for her family. Her trade was barbering, but she could not find a job in that field and instead took a job making $6.00 an hour delivering blood to hospitals. She never dated or even looked for a man to be in her life. God was enough for her and her children. She lived for them and for her God. She never missed Sunday worship and rarely missed Wednesday night Bible study. She sung in the choir and regularly attended every rehearsal. Every Saturday, she supplemented her income by cutting the hair of friends and family.

Angela's rent and utilities combined took all of her money each month, so God had to supply the rest—and supply He did! Her children always had clothes for church and school, and there was more than enough food on the table. Looking back, it couldn't be anything else but God, because Angela never borrowed money or asked the church for help. She raised her children to know and fear the Lord and kept them involved in children and youth ministry until they became adults. Whenever they asked for things she couldn't afford, she never told them, "No." Instead, she responded, "Can you eat it?" It taught them what was really a "need" versus a "want," and they better appreciated what they already had.

I know there had to be times when Angela felt fear or discouragement, or when she was burdened, but never showed it. She always had a peaceful and positive disposition whenever she was in public. She kept moving forward in life, depending on her God every step of the way. Unfortunately, she became extremely ill later in life—but she was strong then, too. I remember going to visit her in the hospital on her birthday. Angela needed a liver transplant, and if she didn't receive it soon, she was going to lose her life. As we were talking, the doctor came in and told her they had a liver and that she was going to be prepped for surgery immediately.

"Look at my God!" she exclaimed. "This is the best birthday present, and only He could give it to me."

Angela received her transplant, and God gave her an additional six years of life. She used that time to love her grandchildren, to serve, and to share God. She cooked dinners for the young adults after church every Sunday. As she neared the end of her life, she often talked about Heaven and what it was going to be like. "If God was this good to me here," she said, "I can only imagine what it is going to be like there!" A couple of weeks before she died, she even made arrangements for her own funeral. She picked the dress, decided how her hair was to be combed, had her nails manicured, and chose who was going to do her makeup. "I'm going to meet Jesus," she insisted, "and I want to look beautiful for Him because I'm going home to be with my God."

As women, we are also designed to be forward-thinking and forward-progressing.

Angela was brave to the end. I sat next to her bedside and sang to her as she took her last breath. I will never forget the courage and strength she exhibited—and I like to think that her and Jochebed are up in Heaven right now, gabbing up a storm (maybe while getting a spiritual spa treatment), and sharing about how faithful God was to them on Earth as they lived out their substance as women, daughters of their King!

WE ARE STRONG TO MOVE PROGRESSIVELY FORWARD: DEBORAH AND RAHAB

As women, we are also designed to be forward-thinking and forward-progressing, and the Bible's premier example of this kind of woman was Deborah. The one thing people always overlook is, while Deborah was a judge and a leader, the Bible first mentions her as being a prophetess and a wife. The inspired Word of God does not bring this out by accident or as an afterthought. This means that her role as a wife was as important to her as her other roles. It also means that her husband, an obscure man named Lapidoth, wasn't threatened by her positions of authority and influence. All of the judges were chosen by God to be leader of the Israelites. Deborah was the only female judge, and she was a phenomenally courageous woman.

"Long before Deborah became a leader in war," wrote Deen, "she was a homemaker. Her house was on the road between Ramah and Beth-el, in the hill country of Ephraim, where flourished olive and palm trees. It was under one of the most royal of date palms that she would sit and give counsel to the people that came to her." (Judges 4:5)

Deborah was also fearless. She was somebody who was driven to be fair as a judge, and she was strong enough to lead the nation's army at a time they needed her the most.

"And she sent and called Barak the son of Abinoam out of Kedeshnaphtali, and said unto him, Hath not the Lord God of Israel commanded, saying, Go and draw toward mount Tabor, and take with thee ten thousand men of the children of Naphtali and of the children of Zebulun? And I will draw unto thee to the river Kishon Sisera, the captain of Jabin's army, with his chariots and his multitude; and I will deliver him into thine hand. And Barak said unto her, If thou wilt go with me, then I will go: but if thou wilt not go with me, then I will not go. And she said, I will surely go with thee: notwithstanding the journey that thou takest shall not be for thine honour; for the Lord shall sell Sisera into the hand of a woman. And Deborah arose, and went with Barak to Kedesh." (Judges 4:6-9)

The reluctant warrior, Barak, wouldn't go to war without her word, even when that word affirmed that Barak was not going to get the glory for the coming victory over Sisera. Instead, the glory would go to a woman—not Deborah, but Jael, a bold woman identified as the wife of Heber the Kenite. She was another woman with strength and courage who was used to help defeat the enemy of God's people. The Lord will use anyone He chooses to carry out His plan, and in this case, He used two powerful women.

To celebrate the victory, the majestic song of Judges 5 was delivered as a powerful praise to God. In it, Deborah is called a mother of Israel, and for good reason. At the time she rose up, the nation was in spiritual lethargy, yet the end result of her nurturing leadership was that the land had rest for forty years (Judges 5:31). All that Deborah did was for her people and for her God. Deborah was a prophetess, wife, judge, counselor, warrior, military leader, and strategist—all in one day. If Deborah could do it, we surely can fill similarly amazing roles with the Lord's help.

Deborah, of course, knew God from her childhood, but God also used another strong, forward-moving woman who did not grow up knowing the God of Israel, although she certainly came to believe in Him later. Rahab used her inner strength to survive her living conditions. (Joshua 2 and 6). Yet she certainly came to believe in Him, and Rahab's extraordinary story showed her entrepreneurship, leadership, knowledge of military strategy, intelligence, and courageousness. Her first identification in the Bible was as a "harlot" (Joshua 2:1), and she lived in the land of Canaan in the city of Jericho, known for its moral depravation. Therefore, it was not seen as socially wrong to be a prostitute there, and Rahab surely used her business savvy to ensure her success in that role.

Joshua 2 tells us Jericho was fortified by a large wall, and her home was built within that wall and located near the front gate, strategically positioned to allow her clients easy access. In a business course I took, the instructor taught us that a successful enterprise had to be in the perfect spot. He said, "location, location, location," and added that your merchandise had to be in demand. Rahab had both the location and the merchandise—and, perhaps through her clientele, she had learned about the Israelites and their God. Rahab also knew how He had helped them conquer their surrounding neighbors, including the powerful Egyptians. She realized as well that God had promised Jericho to the Israelites, who were moving toward them to possess the land. The people of Jericho, of course, were unaware of any of this.

Therefore, when the two Israelite spies came to assess the land and approached her house, Rahab welcomed them in and declared, "For we have heard how the Lord dried up the water of the Red sea for you, when ye came out of Egypt; and what ye did unto the two kings of the Amorites, that were on the other side Jordan, Sihon and Og, whom ye utterly destroyed." (Joshua 2:9b-10) I believe that it is with *this* statement that Rahab declared her faith in God. She said, "*I know* the Lord has given you the land." She believed that the land was theirs because of the Lord's previous actions on their behalf. She was already convinced. Her conversion was based upon the testimonies she'd heard and believed about the God of Israel. There is power in our testimonies, and those Rahab heard utterly changed her life!

The Lord had destroyed some of the strongest nations in the known world, so Rahab understood that Jericho was no match against that kind of power. Then she said, "As soon as we had heard these things, our hearts did melt, neither did there remain any more courage in any man, because of you: for the Lord your God, he is God in heaven above, and in earth beneath." (Joshua 2:11) This declaration was confirmation of Rahab's change of mind, body, and soul. Belief and confession are the only way that someone can become a part of the family of God, and Rahab had at some point already done both—even before the spies arrived at her house. It was because of her belief in God that she aided the spies to ensure they were not going to be captured. She hid them with the stalks of flax drying on her roof. Flax was a plant that was made into linen, and she had enough of it stored to hide the two men. It's likely Rahab, the entrepreneur, also had a business making clothes for herself and other prostitutes and knew how to dye the material to make beautiful garments. After all, it was a red cord, a "scarlet line" (Joshua 2:21) that she later hung in her window.

The spies felt comfortable enough to make a covenant with her to save the lives of both her and her family.

"Now therefore, I pray you, swear unto me by the Lord, since I have shewed you kindness, that ye will also shew kindness unto my father's house, and give me a true token: And that ye will save alive my father, and my mother, and my brethren, and my sisters, and all that they have, and deliver our lives from death. And the men answered her, Our life for yours, if ye utter not this our business. And it shall be, when the Lord hath given us the land, that we will deal kindly and truly with thee." (Joshua 2:12-14)

They trusted that she believed in their God. Her plea to save her family was not made out of self-preservation alone, but out of the faith in God that she shared with them.

Rahab demonstrated her love for her family, a reminder to us that a woman of ill repute can come from a family who cares for her. Prostitutes, and so many other women, may behave shamefully because of sins that were committed against them. Many times, their behavior will be a response to what happened in their past. Detrimental acts committed against them have caused many to turn to drugs, cutting, alcohol, or promiscuity to numb the pain they feel inside. Yet they love their families and others even though they lead a hard life. Even if they are without the love of God in their lives, they have a heart and care about the well-being of others. They cry, they hurt, and they want to give love and to be loved.

Therefore, we should see deeper, beyond the behavior or the sin, and ask God to give us the insight to minister to the very soul of hurting women who are lonely, abandoned, and ostracized—yet *long* to be loved and accepted. While we do not know what led Rahab to become a prostitute, she still had a heart for her family—and her family certainly had a heart for her, even though they had to live separately in her father's house (Joshua 2:12). This is a perfect example of how we need to view people like Rahab. We need to see them as the creation God made, in His image, for this is how God views us. "Above all, have [a] fervent and unfailing love for one another, because love covers a multitude of sins [it overlooks unkindness and unselfishly seeks the best for others]." (1 Peter 4:8, AMP)

> *"Love covers a multitude of sins."*

In helping the two spies, Rahab also gave two commands that showed her military acumen and her leadership qualities. To the men who were looking to capture the spies, she deceived them by instructing them to pursue the spies quickly so they could overtake them (Joshua 2:5). To the spies themselves, she strategically told them to flee to the mountains and remain there for three days until their pursuers returned to the city (Joshua 2:16). She gave this direction, of course, after she had helped them escape by climbing out the window of her advantageously placed home. These strategies worked because Rahab was an intelligent woman with great courage. Additional evidence of this was that the red cord she used to help the spies escape was the same cord that notified the invading Israelite army not to harm her or anyone in her home (Joshua 2:18-20). It's no coincidence that this cord was similar to the sign left for the death angel to pass over the door posts of the house in Egypt, smeared with the scarlet blood of the lamb (Exodus 12:13).

When a woman truly surrenders her heart to God, she becomes "a new creature: old things are passed away; behold, all things are become new." (2 Corinthians 5:17b) Rahab was a changed woman. Even more, God used her to bring about the ultimate miracle, the birth of Jesus Christ. She is mentioned in His genealogy (Matthew 1:5) along with only four other women (Mary His mother, Tamar, Ruth, and Bathsheba). Rahab went on to marry Salmon, an Israelite, and she gave birth to Boaz, the great-grandfather of King David. God used her to bring the Messiah into the world! Her life is a perfect picture of salvation, not just for herself and her family, but for Jew, Gentile, and the entire world. Salvation for all, through the blood of Jesus, came about because of Rahab, and just as her faith saved her and her family from a sentence of death, Jesus saves us from that same sentence (Romans 10:9). "For God so loved the world, that he gave his only begotten Son, that whosoever believeth in him should not perish, but have everlasting life." (John 3:16)

Rahab is one of only two women mentioned, along with Sarah, among the champions of faith in the book of Hebrews. Rahab was the one who "perished not with them that believed not, when she had received the spies with peace." (Hebrews 11:31b) James also identified Rahab as being "justified by works, when she had received the messengers … For as the body without the spirit is dead, so faith without works is dead also." (James 2:25a-26) It was Rahab's faith in God that led her to do what she did—and the same is true for us. Our faith should compel our good deeds for others, and those deeds should glorify the Lord. If they don't glorify Him, even if they are *good*, they are still dead.

How do we know God is getting the glory? When others know that "every good and perfect gift is from above." (James 1:17, NIV) You are that gift—and within you resides the ultimate gift that inspires you to do good. As Matthew 5:16 declares, "In the same way, let your light shine before men, that they may see your good deeds and glorify your Father in heaven." (NIV) He is a good God who loves all and is calling on all to know Him. Even this book is a work, designed to glorify Him in hopes that someone will read it and experience a new or greater walk with Jesus.

Yes, Rahab may have been a harlot—but like my mother used to say, "It is not how you start out that matters the most, but it is how you finish." Rahab finished well. She lived thousands of years ago, and God is still getting the glory today every time her story is told. Prayerfully examine yourself right now. What good works have you done recently? How are they glorifying God?

My heart rejoices as I see God's love towards women. It is exhibited time and again in the Bible. As a wife and mother, Rahab undoubtedly continued to use her strength and intelligence for the forward progression of her family. She made beautiful garments. She maintained her entrepreneurial bent. Transformed by the Lord, she used her skills and gifts for good and God's glory. Notice the undeniable parallels between Rahab's life and the characteristics of the virtuous woman described in Proverbs 31.

- Her husband can safely trust her. (31:11)
- She seeks wool and flax and works willingly with her hands. (31:13)
- She rises early to provide the needs of her family and those who work for her. (31:15)
- She makes profitable financial decisions. (31:16)
- She knows her merchandise is good and works diligently. (31:18)
- She gives to the poor from a sincere heart. (31:20)

- She ensures her family is prepared for the winter and makes their clothing ahead of time. They also are dressed well. (31:21)
- She dresses elegantly with very fine clothing. (31:22)
- Because of her, her husband is well known. (31:23)
- She uses the best materials to provide the best merchandise. (31:24)
- She is clothed with strength and honor and faces each day rejoicing. (31:25)
- She is wise and only has kind words for others. (31:26)
- She is never idle. (31:27)
- Her children and husband think highly of her and call her blessed. (31:28)
- She excels because of her relationship with God. (31:29)
- She is praised by others because of her compassion and hard work that blesses her household and the community. It is all because of her relationship with the Lord. (31:30-31)

A beautiful woman of God once revealed to me how she was molested by her uncle for six years until she was 12 and then raped by her father at age 17. She said her father told her she was "already soiled," so it didn't matter if he had sex with her, too. She felt so dirty that she turned to drugs, alcohol, and prostitution, constantly running, but never getting away from, the pain she felt every day. When she was 18 and saw her molester at her grandfather's funeral, she was angry and made a scene until he left. When confronted by her family, she told them again what he had done to her, to which they replied, "…and look at the way you are dressed now." She felt betrayed and alone because they again abandoned her and protected her violator.

Later, she became addicted to prescription drugs after being hit by a car—yet God preserved her and gave her a chance to seek

Him. She knew about God and at one time even taught Sunday school, but she thought she was too damaged for Him to deliver her. It wasn't until she asked God to take all her mind, body, and soul and completely gave her whole heart to the Lord that she was able to change her friends, alter the places she went, get rid of the drugs, and stop living promiscuously. Jesus came into her heart and changed her life forever.

Today, she understands what it means to have an intimate relationship with God. She feels His love for her, and her heart is now filled with love for Him. She is thankful that she does not look like what she has been through. God preserved her for His use, and she is so excited to see what the next chapter of her life is going to be now that she has God as her Father. Sometimes, she admits that her mind will recall her old lifestyle and she feels unworthy. But reading the Bible, praying, and being around people in church who love God and love her reminds her anew that she is a new creature and that her worth is "far above rubies." (Proverbs 31:10)

What matters is who you are now and who God says you are: His beautiful daughter.

If God did it for her, and if He did it for Rahab, then He'll surely do it for you. God is always there to resurrect anyone who comes to Him and provide them new life, purpose, and rest for their weary soul. It does not matter what you once were or what title people gave you. What matters is who you are now and who God says you are: His beautiful daughter.

WE ARE STRONG TO CARRY OUT OUR PURPOSE AND FULFILL OUR PASSION: TABITHA (DORCAS)

As women of substance, we need to seek God for our purpose and then look even deeper for our passion, because our passion always comes out of our purpose. Passion is easily identified, and God placed that passion within you so that you will know, and begin to walk in the direction of, your purpose. Even more, your purpose will always lead to helping someone else while glorifying the true, living God.

Ask yourself, "What am I passionate about? What gives me the most satisfaction in life?" Whatever the answer—if it helps others and glorifies God, He will take that passion and lead you to your purpose. It's the compass to your success in life! For example, let's say your passion is reading, cooking, or dancing. Read to elderly people in a nursing home or to children in school, in church, or at the library. Cook for the homeless or make dinners for single mothers and fathers. Start an exercise dance class or spend time with special needs children and dance with them for fun. You may be passionate to serve as a councilperson, mayor, nurse, or police officer. Whatever it is, God will turn that passion into a *ministry* that not only meets the needs of others, but will grow to meet your physical, spiritual, emotional, and financial needs as well.

There was a woman in the Bible whose story is brief but fully significant because her passion led to her purpose—and to the miraculous! Her name was Tabitha, also known as Dorcas. Acts 9:36 says that she lived in Joppa, was a disciple of Jesus Christ, and "was excelling in acts of kindness and charity which she did habitually." (NASB) Joppa was located on the coastline, and Bible scholars say many of the women there were widows with children because their husbands were often killed at sea. It is likely Tabitha was one of those widows.

But she wasn't stuck in her situation or debilitated by despair. Instead, Tabitha lived out her passion to help other women who were in the same circumstances as she was. She made clothing for them, and her other works and deeds on their behalf must've been vital and meaningful—for when she became ill and died, the other disciples in Joppa sent for Peter, and the widows were so distraught with grief that they "stood by him weeping, and shewing the coats and garments which Dorcas made, while she was with them." (Acts 9:39b)

Look at what God did next!

"But Peter put them all forth, and kneeled down, and prayed; and turning him to the body said, Tabitha, arise. And she opened her eyes: and when she saw Peter, she sat up. And he gave her his hand, and lifted her up, and when he had called the saints and widows, presented her alive." (Acts 9:40-41)

First of all, Peter sent the widows away. Why? Because of the incredible personal impact Tabitha had on their lives, I believe these widows were beyond grief. They were out of their minds with sorrow and doubt to the point that it was detrimental to the work God was about to perform in their midst. Peter therefore discerned that they had to leave. Next, Peter kneeled, prayed, and turned not toward the body, but away from it. He never looked at the body. He looked toward his God. Death was not his focus, but the Lord was—and Peter *spoke life* to the dead situation. Then he turned toward Tabitha and spoke to her, and the impact of his words was immediate! She opened her eyes and sat up. Glory to God! Even in her death, Tabitha had purpose from the Lord. She was presented alive, "and it was known throughout all Joppa; and many believed in the Lord." (Acts 9:42)

Often as women, when tragedy happens to us, we will tend to just roll up into a ball and wish we could die. Tragedy struck Tabitha when she was widowed, but she didn't do that. She kept busy helping others even in her own pain and loss. She kept living—and so should we. In addition, we need to be like Peter and not approach the dead situations of our lives with hopelessness. In the power of the Holy Spirit, we are to look directly at that circumstance and speak His life to it! We also need to be careful about who we keep company with. If there is someone who is distraught, negative, and filled with doubt—and who is perhaps even facilitating the dead situation in your life—you need to send that person away from you and the circumstance. Why? Because faith and doubt cannot co-exist. Then victory will come in such a miraculous way that only God and God alone will get the praise!

Tabitha's passion led to her purpose—just as it did with me. I remember as a little child when my friends and I played make-believe, I was always the teacher and my friends were the students. I also recall that I had a four-year-old neighbor that I babysat at my home when I was only six. Sure, my five older brothers were there and were actually overseeing both of us, but I was the one playing with and taking care of her. I even made her Kool Aid and an egg salad sandwich every day (after one of my brothers boiled the eggs on the stove).

From my earliest remembrances, my passion was being revealed: I have always loved children and wanted to help them. I get a kick out of kids. Just watching them play gets me all wound up. I can't help myself and naturally get in there with them. In high school, I was involved in all of the future business leader classes and clubs, and when I went to West Valley College in Saratoga near San Jose, I studied toward a degree in business management while working first in retail and then in a bank.

God's favor is a confirmation that allows us to know He is with us.

Yet even in the midst of that, at age 21, I told my sister-in-law, Angela, "One day I'm going to end up opening my own preschool, and it'll be called Genesis Preschool because that's the beginning and the first book in the Bible." Then I added, "And you're going to be the cook," because Angela was skilled in the kitchen.

She looked at me and smiled. "Okay," she said, not exactly sure what to do with my proclamation and career pronouncement for her.

Guess what? For over 26 years, I have been ministering to children through my own business, Genesis Preschool. Angela did indeed become the cook, but more significant is that God brought my purpose and passion to pass—and He was clearly orchestrating everything toward that outcome without my knowledge. By the time I was 30, I was in a career in finance, but my mom couldn't watch my daughter any longer because of her health. I thought, *I'm not leaving my baby to anyone else,* and I decided to leave my job so I could be home to take care of her. By then, I had already launched the children's and youth ministry at my church from infants to young adults. We had a children's church, children's choir, youth bible study, and an entire youth leader and administration ministry, so I was familiar with originating a children's program. Because of my experience with children through the church, God gave me favor with the State of California to open my own childcare program—and that's when Genesis Preschool was born.

God's continued favor allowed me to go back to school and pursue the required bachelor's degree in child and adolescent development, even while already owning the school and serving as its director. God's favor is a confirmation that allows us to know He is with us and that He will open doors that no man or woman can open—but you must knock on the door, knowing that He will make sure it is unlocked for you to walk through. When you are operating in your purpose, God will perform miracles right before your eyes. He will pave the way for you to succeed. All you have to do is get up and go forth.

As my mother used to say, "God blesses what you do." Let my story and Tabitha's example encourage you to *go now* and carry out your purpose in life by fulfilling your passion.

WE ARE STRONG TO FORTIFY OUR STRENGTH THROUGH WORSHIP: THE WOMAN AT THE WELL

Bone is fortified with calcium, which keeps it from becoming brittle and prevents breakage. Because calcium is released into the body, it needs to be replenished by outside sources such as milk, orange juice, and dark, leafy greens. Likewise, a woman of substance needs to be replenished with the strength she gives out to others—and we are fortified in this way through worship. The Holy Spirit of God strengthens us as we worship Him, enabling us to fulfill the purpose He has for us and to bring life to those around us. When we fail to take time to draw near to the Lord, we become bitter, frustrated, and hard to deal with. Our outlook is bleak. We may think we are strong, but just like bones lacking calcium, we become brittle without the power of the Holy Spirit given to us through worship. The difficulties of everyday life break us, much like a stress fracture will do to the physical body, and our strength is weakened from within.

How do we fortify our strength through worship? We must consistently have quiet time with the Lord, getting ourselves alone in a place where we can meditate on who God is—a place where we can be *intimate* with the Lord while communicating with Him through prayer and the Word of God, enhancing our loving relationship with Him. It's only through this intimacy of worship that our relationship with God is validated.

We learn this in the story of the woman of Samaria found in John 4. Better known as the "woman at the well," Jesus meets her in the city of Sychar—and it is amazing how Christ chooses to strategically position Himself at the well in this Samaritan city. In anticipation of the woman's visit, He told His disciples to go away. He didn't want them there because He knew they would have a problem with Him talking to her. Jews did not have dealings with Samaritan people. There was extreme racial hatred, to the point

47

that Jewish people would rather take the longer route when traveling than to pass through Samaria. Not only was she a Samaritan, but she was an outcast as a result of her torrid reputation. This may be one reason why she came to the well in the middle of the day. It was customary for women to draw their water early in the morning while it was cool. She likely came later, in the heat of the day, to avoid the looks and ridicule of the other women. Jesus also understood that the woman wouldn't have been able to express herself as freely as she did if the disciples had been present.

So, Christ was there alone when she arrived to draw water at the well.

> "Jesus said to her, 'Give Me a drink.' For His disciples had gone away into the city to buy food. Then the woman of Samaria said to Him, 'How is it that You, being a Jew, ask a drink from me, a Samaritan woman?' For Jews have no dealings with Samaritans. Jesus answered and said to her, 'If you knew the gift of God, and who it is who says to you, "Give Me a drink," you would have asked Him, and He would have given you living water.' The woman said to Him, 'Sir, You have nothing to draw with, and the well is deep. Where then do You get that living water? Are You greater than our father Jacob, who gave us the well, and drank from it himself, as well as his sons and his livestock?' Jesus answered and said to her, 'Whoever drinks of this water will thirst again, but whoever drinks of the water that I shall give him will never thirst. But the water that I shall give him will become in him a fountain of water springing up into everlasting life.'" (John 4:7-14)

Jesus went to a place that was considered unclean and waited for an unclean woman to offer her the cleansing of His "living water."

That certainly got her attention—and Christ responded by addressing the very issue that caused her true uncleanness before God: intimacy.

> "The woman said to Him, 'Sir, give me this water, that I may not thirst, nor come here to draw.' Jesus said to her, 'Go, call your husband, and come here.' The woman answered and said, 'I have no husband.' Jesus said to her, 'You have well said, "I have no husband," for you have had five husbands, and the one whom you now have is not your husband; in that you spoke truly.'" (John 4:15-18)

Wow! It is absolutely intentional that Jesus spoke to this particular woman who had a problem with intimacy—because intimacy is at the center of worship! When looking at biblical truths, there is always a physical parallel with the spiritual. Just as the physical intimacy of sexual intercourse between a man and a woman consummates a marriage, to be a woman of substance, you must have that *same encounter spiritually* with the Lord, and God desires to have this intimate relationship with you.

It is amazing how Jesus broke all the rules to get to her. He crossed city limits and defied racial prejudice, gender barriers, religious differences, and cultural divides. Jews would never enter Samaria because they saw it as unclean. They considered the people to be a mixed breed and a deviation from Jewish purity. Samaritan women were insignificant and nothing more than property. They had no rights and no voice. It was improper for a Rabbi to have any dealings with a Samaritan female, especially one with her lifestyle. The Samaritans worshiped in one place and the Jews worshiped in another place, and they had different views on how to worship God. The cultural differences between the two, brought on by the mixture of the races and paganism, was adopted due to the siege and captivity that took place there in 722 B.C.

But Jesus did not let any of these barriers hinder Him from getting to this woman—

and He is just as determined to reach each one of us today. John 4:23 says He is seeking out those who are willing to worship Him. Through the living water Christ offered, the Holy Spirit would enter into the woman at the well, and she would experience intimacy with God. This is the true worship "in spirit and in truth" that Jesus proclaimed to her in John 4:23 before revealing Himself as the Mes-

We have to establish and maintain an intimate relationship with God first.

siah. But for the woman at the well to receive His living water and enjoy that intimacy, she was going to have to first confront her physical intimacy issues. She longed for intimacy, but she was going about it the wrong way.

We as women tend to do that, so we have to flip the script and learn to approach intimacy the right way. We have to establish and maintain an intimate relationship with God first. Jesus said to the woman, "You spoke truly!" We have to be honest about ourselves and what's in our lives, too. Whatever it is that's hindering us from growing in the Lord and being intimate with Him, we need to be truthful about it with ourselves and with God. He's not going to beat us down about it. He simply wants us to acknowledge it so that we can overcome it, be victorious over it, and get closer to Him so it won't be in the way of Him approaching us.

The woman at the well did exactly that. The Bible doesn't record the rest of the conversation that happened between her and Jesus before the disciples returned and she departed, but it must've been life-altering—because she went into the city and told everyone she could about Christ. Not only does this worship experience with the Lord establish a more intimate relationship with Him, but it also strengthens you and gives you the courage to face your fears as well as provides personal assurance that God is *real*. Just as sexual intimacy produces an offspring, so does the worship experience with God.

The woman went into town and told everyone, the very people she had been avoiding, to come see Jesus, the man who told her everything about herself. The living water was now hers, her spiritual intimacy with the Lord was underway, and she couldn't help but declare her love for God! Many believed—and a birth of new believers sprung forth from her witness compelled by her worship.

Just as a marriage is fortified through sexual intimacy, our relationship with God is fortified through intimate worship with Him. I have a special place in my home where I can be alone to meet the lover of my soul. It has pillows, a mat, and a blanket that reads, "The steadfast love of the Lord never ceases; his mercies never come to an end; they are new every morning." (Lamentations 3:22-23, ESV) During my intimate time with the Lord, I light candles and play soft worship music, and then I lay prostrate (face down on the ground in total submission and reverence) before Him. I tell my loving God how much I love and trust Him, and I praise Him that everything that is good in my life is because of Him. Next, I make my requests known unto Him by speaking those vulnerable things that are in my heart. Sometimes I simply let the worship music minister to my soul, and that helps me to then enter into a worship experience with my God.

I do this every morning before I start my day. Before I speak to anyone else, I speak to God. The Holy Spirit always ministers to me and strengthens me to be able to face whatever challenges come that day. He is ever faithful when I am faithful to fortify my strength through worship.

The method you choose to have your worship time with your God is up to you. But as a woman of substance, you must stay in constant communication with your God in order to maintain your strength in the Lord.

The Substance of a Woman

❖ ❖ ❖

We've discovered that bone is the first of the two substances that make up women according to the biblical account of her creation by God from Adam. The bone makes us strong so we can protect life, move progressively forward, carry out our purpose and fulfill our passion, and it gives us more power to fortify our strength through worship. We've enjoyed the stories of women from Scripture who personified these incredible traits that God has endowed upon every woman who serves Him.

But there is a second substance that reveals the softer side of women—and it is glorious.

Chapter 4

"And the Lord God caused a deep sleep to fall
upon Adam, and he slept: and he took one of his ribs,
and closed up the flesh instead thereof; And the rib,
which the Lord God had taken from man, made
he a woman, and brought her unto the man."
(Genesis 2:21-23)

Inside the bone is the marrow, a soft, gel-like substance which produces the blood cells that carry life throughout our body. Although bone is a hard substance, we must understand as women that we cannot be hard all the time. There is a soft, emotional side to us that must be protected and nurtured in order for us to function the way God originally intended—and it is from this side where our life flows outward to everyone in our lives.

WE ARE SOFT TO NURTURE OTHERS AND TO RECEIVE NURTURING: ELIZABETH

Her name says it all: Elizabeth means, "God is my oath" or "God is my promise," and she is introduced to us in Luke 1. She lived in a time when Judea was ruled by the tyrannical and deranged King Herod, the same Herod who made the decree to kill all the boys in Bethlehem and its vicinity who were two years old and under because he felt his throne was threatened. She also lived during the time that God had not spoken to His people for 400 years.

Yet none of this undermined Elizabeth's faith. She still served the Lord. As we learned earlier, as an elder, Elizabeth's mentor-type friendship and praise-centered presence was the main reason Mary made it through one of the toughest times in her life after discovering she was pregnant with God's Son.

The Bible shows us that Elizabeth was a devout woman of God. She descended from the priestly line of Aaron, and she lived an upright, righteous life by following every commandment and ordinance. She remembered commandments such as honoring the Sabbath to keep it holy, she did not steal or kill, she did not covet her neighbor's goods, and she did not commit adultery. Elizabeth also observed ordinances such as the Passover, the Feast of Unleavened Bread, the Feast of Tabernacles, and circumcision ceremonies. Scripture describes her as blameless (Luke 1:6), meaning there were no rumors of her gossiping about people, doing wrong to them, or having a bad attitude. She was fair and just in her dealings with others. No one could say anything unpleasant about her.

But Elizabeth had a condition that left her ostracized and marginalized in her culture: she couldn't bear a child. The Bible says she was stricken in years (Luke 1:7, 18), meaning she was likely over 80 years old. She was well past child-bearing years, and her husband Zechariah was as old as she. Yet she constantly sought God about her barrenness, which the people considered to be a curse from the Lord. Even the angel of the Lord that appeared to Mary called Elizabeth "barren." Every day, people reminded her of her inability to get pregnant, and most thought it must be because of some type of unconfessed sin in her life, since she had no children despite her advanced age. Even now, others will often make assumptions about you with no idea that God is working something miraculous in your life.

Since she was the wife of a priest, I can imagine her attending one circumcision ceremony after another, nurturing every mother who came with her son. Elizabeth's focus was to please her God, and she and her husband were both committed to the ministry of the Lord to His people. She found her peace and rest in God, and this made her soft in spirit so she could sensitively minister to others despite her inner pain.

Like Elizabeth, you may be dealing with and praying about some sort of barrenness. "Barren" refers to a place that is dry, sterile, and incapable of producing life. Your barren situation may involve your marriage or a divorce, a rebellious child, a financial struggle, or your physical and mental health. It could be even something deeper: your insecurities, loneliness, anxiety, or broken heart. Because of these things, people may see you as being incomplete or less than you should be. But even in your own hurt, fears, and doubts, and even through feeling disgraced by others, you can remain faithful to your God. That's what Elizabeth did, and it kept her through all the disappointments in her life. Her steadfast commitment to and love for God did not allow her own personal pain to get in the way of her service to Him.

It is both possible and useful to minister to others while you are in pain. I have seen and done it myself by attending worship service every Sunday, singing in the choir, ushering, teaching, attending Bible study, helping the poor, and visiting and praying with the sick and elderly—all while dealing with barren issues. A nurturing ministry to others is part of the healing process for your own barren situation. Somehow, that barrenness takes a back seat to the joy of doing the will of the Father. Don't stay focused on the problem. Stay focused on the problem solver, God, and trust in His promise to take care of your future. As Jeremiah 29:11 assures, "'For I know the plans I have for you,' declares the Lord, 'plans to prosper you and not to harm you, plans to give you hope and a future.'" (NIV)

He certainly took care of Elizabeth. The angel of the Lord came to Zechariah, even as he was faithfully ministering by the altar of incense, and told him something incredible.

"Do not be afraid, Zechariah; your prayer has been heard. Your wife Elizabeth will bear you a son, and you are to call him John. He will be a joy and delight to you, and many will rejoice because of his birth, for he will be great in the sight of the Lord." (Luke 1:13-15a)

What an honor! God chose Elizabeth to be the recipient of His first miracle after four centuries of silence! Reminiscent of what He did for Abraham and Sarah in the ancient past, the Lord brought life to a dead womb. Only God can do such a miracle. He specializes in bringing dead situations back to life.

He specializes in bringing dead situations back to life.

But there was more! Not only did he give Elizabeth the baby she was praying for, but he also gave her the child who was going to announce the coming Messiah and call the people to repentance while paving the way for the Savior of the world. God did exceedingly, abundantly, above all Elizabeth could ask or think (Ephesians 3:20). All the time she was praying, God had a plan for Elizabeth. He knew He could trust her, and only her, with that plan. She had never complained or turned her back on God but continued in her love for Him—positioning herself to be used of the Lord to manifest His miracle-working power, for "with God nothing shall be impossible." (Luke 1:37)

We must trust in God's plan and believe in His Word while we are waiting for the manifestation of His promises. If Elizabeth was here, she'd tell you it was all worth the wait! After all, "they that wait upon the Lord shall renew their strength; they shall mount up with wings as eagles; they shall run, and not be weary; and they shall walk, and not faint." (Isaiah 40:31) Rest in the Lord and trust in Him. "Wait on the Lord: be of good courage, and he shall strengthen thine heart: wait, I say, on the Lord." (Psalm 27:14)

Luke 1:24 tells us that Elizabeth hid herself away for five entire months and took time apart from everyone and everything while she rested from her duties and cares of life to have sweet communion with her God. In the end, Luke 1:25 tells us Elizabeth received the words of the angel and declared, "Thus hath the Lord dealt with me in the days wherein he looked on me, to take away my reproach among men." In other words, she proclaimed that God had vindicated her name!

No longer could others call her "barren" Elizabeth. They would now call her Elizabeth the *mother* of John.

God is always looking on you. Do not allow people to label you. Hold your head up and refuse to be defined by others. Instead, allow God to define who you are because only He knows your end. You are the daughter of the Most High God! You are who God says you are, you can do what God says you can do, you can be what God says you can be, and you will have what God says you can have. Whatever the barren situation in your life, God has an answer for it. You are more than your situation, so don't count yourself out. Elizabeth's story proves it's never too late.

Even as Elizabeth was used of the Lord to nurture others, we must also receive nurturing. We are emotional beings, so if we do not take the time to receive both physically and spiritually, then we become hard and brittle and begin to break. It's reciprocal: as much as we give out, we must get back.

One of the main ways we nurture ourselves is through rest—and this was ordained by God. In Genesis 2:1-3, after God completed the work of creating Heaven and Earth, He took the seventh day to rest as an example He wants us to follow. It is vital for us as women to rest in Him and take time to be at peace from the cares of this life. This means we are to cease from the work that we do on a daily basis. The sabbath is to be a time of peace and joy in the Lord where we focus on Him. It is also a time to put your *will* at rest—the things that you want to do—and to give those things to the Lord. God instituted this day of rest for our benefit and the replenishment of our physical, spiritual, emotional, and mental health. Jesus affirmed this in Mark 2:27 when He said, "The sabbath was made for man, and not man for the sabbath."

Taking the time to get a massage, enjoy a makeover at the cosmetics counter at the mall, have a spa getaway for a manicure and pedicure, or to rent a hotel room so you can order room service and sleep for as long as you want are superb ways to rest. More active ideas are golfing, swimming, or hiking, all with the goal of leaving the cares of life at home and replenishing yourself.

We nurture others through trusting and authentic relationships with one another. I have a friend, Olivia, with whom I can be myself. We joke and laugh all the time. We take walks and kidingly talk about how to solve all of the problems of the world. We take trips and worship God together. Although we attend different churches, we make time to nurture one another. I do not have to minister to her, but we usually end up mutually ministering to each other.

For pastor's wives, it is very lonely. T.D. Jakes says pastor's wives are the loneliest people in the world, and that is so true. It's hard for us to find someone we can be themselves with, so I value my friend, Olivia McPhearson, who I have known since junior high school. I'm a pastor's wife. She's both a deacon's wife and a deacon herself. We both love the Lord and work diligently in our churches, but we take that time to be free with each other. You only need one friend. It's so refreshing.

WE ARE SOFT TO LAUGH, PLAY, AND TOUCH: REBEKAH

As women, we will sometimes isolate ourselves, and too much isolation is not good for us. We must be with others. It is important to our spiritual and emotional growth. God knows it is not good for us to be alone. He saw that with Adam in the Garden when He gave him Eve, and he saw it with the patriarchs of our faith. Abraham had Sarah—and Isaac was given Rebekah.

Rebekah was an extraordinary woman who was chosen by God Himself to be Isaac's wife. The way she was set apart by the Lord was profound. The chief servant of Abraham was told to go to Abraham's homeland to find Isaac a wife. The servant not only made an oath to Abraham to do it, but he also asked God to guide him to the right woman. He prayed about his mission.

This is vital for us as women because we have many life missions that can at times seem so overwhelming that fear of failure can try to overtake our souls. We have responsibilities on the job, we are mothers to our children, and we serve in church ministry. Like Abraham's servant, we must seek God's help for insight and strength for these missions. We will be faced with tasks that we may not feel qualified to fulfill, but God is available and waiting for us to call on Him for help. When we do, He will equip us with all we need to accomplish what He has given us to do.

This is what Abraham's servant did when he needed to fulfill his duty of finding a wife for Isaac. He arrived at the town of Nahor in the early evening, and he prayed.

> "Lord, God of my master Abraham, make me successful today, and show kindness to my master Abraham. See, I am standing beside this spring, and the daughters of the townspeople are coming out to draw water. May it be that when I say to a young woman, 'Please let down your jar that I may have a drink,' and she says, 'Drink, and I'll water your camels too'—let her be the one you have chosen for your servant Isaac. By this I will know that you have shown kindness to my master." (Genesis 24:12-14, NIV)

The servant asked both for success and for a sign so that he'd know beyond a shadow of a doubt who God had selected for Isaac. It's good and appropriate for us to request a sign from the Lord to ensure we are doing His will and not our own. But do you see the sign the servant requested? He asked for it to be the woman who was going to offer water to him *and* to his camels. He sought a woman of quality character.

Enter Rebekah with her jar on her shoulder. Scripture declares that she was very beautiful. She answered the servant's request for water, then offered to draw water for his camels—and "without saying a word, the man watched her closely to learn whether or not the Lord had made his journey successful." (Genesis 24:21, NIV) When the camels had finished drinking, the servant learned she was the daughter of Abraham's sister-in-law, and he knew God had answered his prayer. Rebekah was the one!

She was generous, compassionate, and able to see a need and meet it. She also had a heart to go beyond what was requested of her, and she was hard working because it took several trips to draw enough water from the well to care for the camels. She had a gentle spirit toward the servant who was a complete stranger to her. Clearly, Rebekah was beautiful on the inside as well—the kind of woman who was going to bring the favor of the Lord to a husband as Proverbs 18:22 proclaims: "Whoso findeth a wife findeth a good thing, and obtaineth favour of the Lord." Finally, Rebekah was a soft, gentle woman who had been taught to be that way from her mother.

God equips you to be a wife through the influence of older women. I remember when I first met my husband's Grandma Ruby. Derek was still my fiancé at the time, and she was a devout woman of God and the mother of her church. She asked me to come to the dining area to set the table for dinner. That was not a problem for me. My mother, Vernell, was a stickler about table-setting etiquette. When Grandma Ruby came in and saw the table properly set, she said to my future husband, "This one here is a keeper. She is a good woman from a good family. You better treat her with the highest respect."

I was amazed. I had just met her and had hardly spoken to her, yet she discerned the type of woman I was. At the end of the visit, she took me aside. "I had you set the table to see what kind of woman you were," she revealed. "I knew if you could set a table that there was a good woman teaching you—and that you would be a good wife for my grandson." At that moment, I was so grateful for my mother's influence. I did not understand that by teaching me proper table etiquette she was also positioning me to become a wife that brought God's honor to a man. It is just as 1 Peter 3:3-4 says.

> "What matters is not your outer appearance—the styling of your hair, the jewelry you wear, the cut of your clothes—but your inner disposition. Cultivate inner beauty, the gentle, gracious kind that God delights in. The holy women of old were beautiful before God that way, and were good, loyal wives to their husbands." (MSG)

Rebekah accompanied Abraham's servant and became just that kind of wife to Isaac. Even more, she was a wife who understood the value of taking time to laugh, play, and have fun with her husband. Genesis 26:8 says that Isaac and Rebekah were caught by the king of the Philistines laughing and flirting with each other. He knew that Rebekah was Isaac's wife and not his sister because it was obvious in the way they engaged with one another. This is healthy for a marriage, and it is vital to the life of a woman and the relationship of her marriage. It shows love and the ability to let all the cares of the world go and be intimate outside of sexual intimacy.

For the single woman, it is just as important to engage in a relaxing, carefree time with your like-minded friends. You need a person whose company you enjoy and with whom you can give and receive advice, someone you trust with your innermost secrets and fears and who will pour the same type of vulnerability and trust back into you. This person can be a sibling or an extended family member like a cousin, as well as a friend. It can also be someone of the opposite sex, whom you join in a group to attend a movie or to go to dinner or church events with or whom you just talk to on the phone, that fulfills the longing for companion-ship. Be careful, though, that any opposite sex relationship remain strictly platonic. If you sense it becoming anything more than that, you must exercise caution. You do not want to find yourself in a position where you sin against God by having sexual relations outside of marriage. Remember, this is a time of refreshing and reflecting on the goodness of God in your life. Keep the focus on this being a special time for yourself. You do not want to add sin, guilt, and resentment that will undermine your ability to rest.

If the male friend in your life becomes more than a friend, it's a good thing because you have established a healthy relation-ship first by getting to know each other. Set boundaries and, if you begin discussing marriage, commit to a premarital counseling class. In your dating relationship, make sure you still take time for yourself to be alone for physical, spiritual, and mental refreshing.

WE ARE SOFT TO GIVE AND RECEIVE ACCEPTANCE AND AFFIRMATION: THE "SINFUL" WOMAN

Women who give of themselves to others also need to receive love, affection, and acceptance. It is so important for women to have people in their lives that show love toward them and accepts them for who they are and not what people expect them to be. Often, we try to portray an image to others that is not always who we actually are but rather what people expect it of us so we can fit in. But all of us are individuals who need to embrace ourselves and accept who we are. We are nurtured and replenished when people accept us that way and do not expect us to be like everyone around us.

It is so important for women to have people in their lives that show love toward them and accepts them for who they are.

When Jesus was invited to a dinner in the home of a Pharisee named Simon in Luke 7:36-50, they were joined by a woman of the city who was a sinner, likely the town prostitute. She was there to see Jesus and brought with her an alabaster box of ointment. In biblical times, perfumes and oil were expensive, treasured, and only used for special occasions (or, in her case, as a necessity of her profession). Therefore, the act of using the pricey oil was a huge statement of her appreciation for Jesus and for whatever it was that He had already done for her previously. She had to have met Jesus before this, and He must've done something very special for her to come into Simon's home. Whatever it was, through her gesture, she was saying to Christ, "You are worthy of all that I have and all that I am." She used the contents of the box to show her deep love and appreciation for Him by wetting his feet with her tears, wiping them with her hair, and kissing and anointing his feet with the oil.

To wash someone's feet was a display of the utmost humility, submission, and gratitude. In the woman's eyes, Jesus' feet were the most beautiful sight in the room, but what's also interesting is that she noticed his feet were dirty at all. Why would she notice this? It was customary in Jesus' day for the host to wash the feet of his guest when someone entered the home. But Simon the Pharisee had not washed Christ's feet. I can imagine her thoughts. *How could the*

One who showed such love toward me be treated in such a manner?
It makes me sorrowful to see Jesus treated with such disrespect.

She responded by washing His feet herself with the tears from her own body, an incredibly personal act. The kisses she softly placed on His feet were a demonstration of her love for Him. Furthermore, lacking a towel to dry his feet, she used her very own hair, a symbol of her glory, dignity, and honor (1 Corinthians 11:15). In those times, a woman's hair was only to be seen by her husband. Only prostitutes displayed their hair in public. Yet for her, nothing was too extravagant for Jesus! She was showing to everyone present that Jesus had become the one and only intimate relationship she'd ever have from that day forward and that she was willing to give her glory to Him. It was a sign of total submission for her to use her hair to dry Christ's feet, as though she was expressing, *You can have all of me, even the very hairs on my head.* To her, this act was like a wedding ceremony, a true display of love and worship.

Then, to top off her loving act, she anointed His feet with the expensive oil, signifying His deity. In the Bible, oil is a symbol of the Holy Spirit. This woman went above and beyond what was required and exhibited complete homage to the One who could forgive her sins. This was a true example of the scriptural exhortation to love the Lord your God with all your heart, mind, soul, and strength (Matthew 22:37).

Because of her sinful reputation, the others in the room did not even look at her, much less move to touch her. Yet she did not care who was there, what they thought of her, or how they felt about her. She yielded her will over to Jesus and put her spirit at rest in Christ's love for her. She let go of the cares and burdens of her life in that moment and focused on the One who could give her peace.

Though Jesus knew her way of life, He did not judge her. He

had compassion on her. He saw the intent of her heart and her desire to worship Him. She gave Jesus the acceptance and affirmation He did not receive from His host, and He not only returned both of those to her—He forgave her sins (Luke 7:48).

Her loving act glorified Jesus to everyone present, and it shows that when we place the emphasis on God in everything we do and make what we do "all about Him," in His eyes it really becomes all about *us*. He has all we need—peace of mind, security, protection—and He derives pleasure in giving those blessings to us as a byproduct of bringing glory to Him.

WE ARE SOFT TO TAKE CARE OF OURSELVES WITH NUTRITION AND REST: ESTHER

Just as the marrow produces the blood that the body needs to live, we must do and receive the physical things that help us to continue to exist. Nutrition and rest are essential. In the book of Esther, when the women were to come before the king, they were sent through a time of purification so that they could look and be their best when they met the king. Esther went through this purification and eventually was chosen by the king to be his wife. This picture of purification is an example of obtaining rest for the physical body. Just as Esther went through a period of beautification to prepare her for the ultimate encounter with the king, rest will do the same for us. It replenishes us to be able to do the work that God created us to do and helps us to live out His purpose for our lives.

The purification process, or beauty treatments, that Esther received prior to going before the king consisted of six months of oils, including myrrh, for massaging of the skin, and six months of perfumes and cosmetics. These extensive treatments were well worth it to ensure the well-being of each woman who went before the king. Although we may not be able to do a year-long beauty treatment, we should certainly take one day each week to care for the well-being of our mind, body, and soul. God requires this of us because He knows what we need, and He cares about us. What a wonderful God He is who takes time to think about *us*.

In the story of Esther, we meet an orphaned slave girl destined by God to become the queen of the most powerful nation in the world at that time, the Persian Empire.

> *What a wonderful God He is who takes time to think about us.*

Hadessah was her Hebrew name, which means "myrtle tree," while her Persian name is translated as "star." Raised by her cousin Mordecai, Esther was born in a period of captivity that had begun over 100 years prior when her Hebrew ancestors were taken into captivity by King Nebuchadnezzar after they disobeyed God. Therefore, Esther had to deal with discrimination, poverty, racism, sexism, and oppression because her people were despised and treated with contempt. Since she lost both of her parents, Esther was considered, along with widows, to be among the most vulnerable people in biblical times. The Israelites were told to make provision for the poor, which included orphans and widows, when they reaped a harvest (Leviticus 19:10). James 1:27 also exhorts us to care for the parentless and widows as evidence of having a pure and undefiled religion before God.

Many like Esther were forced into slavery and exploited because they had no protection, but the Lord provided for her by having Mordecai adopt her. She did not allow her harsh conditions to break her spirit. She trusted in her God and maintained a spirit of beauty. Not only was she lovely on the outside, but she was beautiful on the inside. It was that inner attractiveness that gained her favor with the chamberlain, the king, and everyone she met (Esther 2:9, 15, 17). It is our inward attitude and faith that gives us favor with our King and brings Him delight. God is looking for us to portray a reflection of who He is, and when He sees this in us,

He is pleased. The Lord expects us to nurture these qualities on the inside even more so than our outward appearance. We as women spend more time on our looks because that is what is emphasized in our society, but what is acceptable to God is our inner self—our character traits of honesty, love, compassion, kindness, and unselfishness.

The fruit of the Holy Spirit in Galatians 5—love, joy, peace, longsuffering, gentleness, goodness, faith, meekness, and self-control—were undeniably evident in Esther's life, as was her compassion for others and her confident, positive outlook. Our attitude toward life should be just as assured and optimistic because we have a Savior who died so that we may have life and have it more abundantly (John 10:10). Your God is able to keep you, no matter who left you, no matter the gravity of the loss of your loved one, no matter the diagnosis, and no matter the lack of money, the eviction or foreclosure notice, or the pink slip. Don't allow your circumstances to change your disposition. Instead, as God declares in Psalm 46:10, "Be still, and know that I am God; I will be exalted among the nations, I will be exalted in the earth." (NIV) What you believe about God and about yourself will determine how well you face adversity. Your troubles will either make you better, or they will make you bitter.

The king chose Esther, she became queen, and he loved her deeply (Esther 2:17). But even with her position and her connection to the king, she still had to deal with the issues of life. She learned from Mordecai that her people faced genocide because of prejudice against them—and Mordecai told her she was the only one who could save them. God had placed her as queen "for such a time as this" (Esther 4:14) to help her people. She respected Mordecai and his instruction to go to the king about the threat, but it was not customary for the queen to approach the king unless he summoned her. To do otherwise was a death sentence, but Esther courageously called for a three-day fast for all the Jewish people while she prepared to go to the king, proclaiming, "I will go in unto the king, which is not according to the law: and if I perish, I perish." (Esther 4:16)

When you are faced with tough situations in life, fasting and prayer is the best practice to strengthen you spiritually and give you clarity about God's will. Esther 5 lays out the plan God gave her as a result of her fast and her faith. That plan unraveled the plot against her people, rescued them from certain death, and kept her in the king's favor. She became the shining star in the entire land, and God's deliverance was a sign of His everlasting covenant with His people. This covenant was symbolized by the myrtle tree (one meaning of Esther's name) in Isaiah 55:13, which says, "Instead of the thorn shall come up the fir tree, and instead of the brier shall come up the myrtle tree: and it shall be to the Lord for a name, for an everlasting sign that shall not be cut off."

Although God is never specifically mentioned in the story of Esther, His providence is evident throughout it. Just as we were once captive to sin through the disobedience of Adam, Jesus came to deliver us from that bondage and the death sentence that it brought. Esther inherited captivity through the disobedience of her ancestors but was delivered from possible death through her trust in God. Galatians 5:1 tells us, "Stand fast therefore in the liberty wherewith Christ hath made us free, and be not entangled again with the yoke of bondage." Therefore, we must be intentionally aware that because of our freedom in Jesus Christ, we are no longer to revert to our old ways of thinking and doing things that will place us back in bondage. God has given us the liberty to live in victory—and seeking Him for guidance and wisdom is the way we remain victorious.

The adoption of Esther by Mordecai symbolizes the adoption of the Gentiles into the royal family of God. Romans 8:15 declares, "For ye have not received the spirit of bondage again to fear; but ye have received the Spirit of adoption, whereby we cry, Abba, Father." We were orphaned just like Esther through the inheritance of sin, but God became our Father through Christ. We have been purified through the blood of Jesus which enables us to go boldly to the throne of God. There, we obtain mercy and grace when we need help (Hebrews 4:16), just as Esther was able to go to the king to obtain mercy for her people. We were saved from an eternal death sentence by Christ's death on the cross and His resurrection from the dead. His sacrifice assures God's everlasting covenant with us (John 3:16), just as the Jewish people were spared because of Esther's petition to the king. Once again, the Lord used a woman to demonstrate His plan of salvation.

God understands our importance, and time and again that is exhibited throughout the Bible. We must understand how important we are as women, just as God continues to substantiate our being. Titus 2:11-14 tells us.

> "For the grace of God that bringeth salvation hath appeared to all men, Teaching us that, denying ungodliness and worldly lusts, we should live soberly, righteously, and godly, in this present world; Looking for that blessed hope, and the glorious appearing of the great God and our Saviour Jesus Christ; Who gave himself for us, that he might redeem us from all iniquity, and purify unto himself a peculiar people, zealous of good works."

Now that we've explored who we are in God—from the way God thoughtfully and artistically created women to our bone-like strengths and marrow-like softness—we are ready to discover something just as astonishing: how incredibly important we are to Him.

PART TWO

How Important We Are to God

Chapter 5

"But even the very hairs of your head are all numbered.
Fear not therefore: ye are of more value than many sparrows."
(Luke 12:7)

I'll never forget the day I found out how important I was to God. I was 21 years old, it was New Year's Eve, and for the second consecutive year I was in charge of putting together a party at my cousin's house in Stockton, California, about an hour and a half from where I lived in San Jose with my parents. I had completed all the prep work: the deejay was hired and the food and drinks were being provided by a caravan of family and friends driving in from San Jose. It was going to be *the* event to ring in the New Year.

All of us had decided to leave for Stockton by four o'clock so that we could beat the dense fog we knew was soon going to roll in and impede our driving. When my cousin called at two o'clock to make sure all was well, I told her we would be on our way in a couple of hours.

Then, right before four, God spoke to me. It was out of nowhere. His words were unmistakable and His command simple.

"This day, you will go to church."

I began to cry. I knew it was the Lord—and I felt so unworthy. "How could the God of the universe take time to talk to me? Why would He even want to talk to me?" But even as those questions crossed my mind, peace swept over my soul. I dried my tears. My mind was made up. I *had* heard the voice of the Lord, and I *was* going to obey.

I called my cousin and told her I wasn't coming to the party I had organized. "You all will have to go on without me."

I could tell by her voice that she was not happy. "What could have happened within two hours?" she accused. "I just talked to you."

I told her—and after a pause, she conceded. "Okay, but I don't know what to do."

"I cannot help you. God is calling on me, and I have to answer."

That evening was the "Watch Night" service at my father's church, San Jose Missionary Baptist. I was a member and had gone to church there since I was a little girl, but I hadn't yet given my life over to Jesus Christ. In fact, I had recently started dabbling with alcohol and going out to night clubs. I was even dating a young man who was a drug dealer, and it didn't bother me. Satan was setting a trap for me—and I was finally starting to realize it, especially after what had happened with my mother, Vernell, the day before when I asked her to go to the mall with me to see a dress I wanted. It was a gorgeous, slinky, black-laced dress that was backless and cut low in the front. It came to right above my knee and was very form-fitting. I didn't have enough money and hoped she would buy it for me, maybe so I could wear it to the New Year's Eve party.

I tried it on, and when I walked out of the dressing room to model it for her, I suddenly felt like the walls were closing in around me.

I had never seen my mother look at me the way she did when she saw me in that dress.

"I will not be a part of this," she said, her voice sad and disappointed. Her eyes pierced through me from below her scrunched brow, and her lips were pressed together into a partial frown. "I will *not* buy that dress for you." She then grabbed her purse, got up from the chair, and walked out.

That horrible image—and her disappointment that haunted

me throughout the night before—returned to my mind once more as I walked up to her. She was in her bedroom.

"Mom," I said, "God came to me in my room, just moments ago. He told me that I will go to church tonight. I already called and told everyone I'm not going to the party."

She started crying. "You have to listen to the Lord," she said—then, like Elizabeth with Mary, she started praising God and calling out to Him. I don't know if she'd been praying ever since she saw me in that dress, but based on the way she was acting, I imagine she had been. Dad didn't know anything about what was happening. He was in his office preparing for service that evening, and when he was in there, we knew not to disturb him.

> *"You have to listen to the Lord."*

When I entered our storefront church, there was no vestibule, so I walked right into the sanctuary. As I came further inside, my dad saw me and was at my side before I could sit down. He instantly laid his hands on me and prayed. I was immediately slain in the Holy Spirit. This manifestation simply didn't happen in Baptist churches, so I had never seen it before, much less experienced it. I stayed on the floor flat on my back for half the service, my arms stretched taut toward the ceiling. I could hear the voice of my mighty Lord the entire time I was slain, and I was also aware that my father had returned to the pulpit and that the Spirit was moving powerfully. The entire church was praising God.

It was unusual. It was miraculous. It was wonderful. Right then, it was as though God stamped His seal in my heart—and from that night forward my life has been committed to the Lord. I dropped the boyfriend, stopped going to clubs, and never drank again. At the advent of the New Year, I was given new life in Christ—and it was *the* event of my life.

God chose me that day, and I am so grateful I answered the call and still answer His call today. I think of Psalm 8:4. "What is man, that thou art mindful of him?" Then I revise it to say, "...mindful of *me*?" It's incredible, but I have felt the constant love and protection of Jesus since then. I am so thankful for His miraculous deliverance and conversion in my life. I knew I had purpose and that God loved me greatly, and over the years He has repeatedly shown me who—and Whose—I am.

It's when we understand how significant we are to God that we begin to live out our true purpose in life. We will continue to face difficult circumstances and challenges in life. We will have ups and downs, joy and sadness. But God will go through it all with us.

There are two chapters of the book of Psalms that speak to us about how important we are to the Lord: Psalm 8 and Psalm 139. They are both attributed to David. The first one gives praise to God and the astonishing mindfulness He has toward us, while the second is a prayer to the Lord to examine our hearts and see our true devotion to Him. Let's take a look at each one of these remarkable passages, with an eye on what they say to us about our substance as women.

PSALM 8: THE GOD WHO HAS GIVEN YOU AUTHORITY

"O Lord, our Lord, how excellent is thy name in all the earth! who hast set thy glory above the heavens. Out of the mouth of babes and sucklings hast thou ordained strength because of thine enemies, that thou mightest still the enemy and the avenger. When I consider thy heavens, the work of thy fingers, the moon and the stars, which thou hast ordained; What is man, that thou art mindful of him? and the son of man, that thou visitest him? For thou hast made him a little lower than the angels, and hast crowned him with glory and honour. Thou madest him to have dominion over the works of thy hands; thou hast put all things under his feet: All sheep and oxen, yea, and the beasts of the field; The fowl of the air, and the fish of the sea, and whatsoever passeth through the paths of the seas. O Lord our Lord, how excellent is thy name in all the earth!" (Psalm 8:1-9)

Here, David wrote about God's excellence and revealed how much we mean to Him as the Lord's ambassadors, His representatives on Earth. We discover that God has given us authority over His creation, and that His thoughts are forever toward us. As women, we have the added ability through Him to procreate and bring new life into the world, just as He created life with Adam and Eve. We are to be the evidence that there is a true and living God who created the Earth and everything that dwells in it and proclaim His glory through our faith and life in Him.

In the Bible, **Anna** was one of His ambassadors—a devout woman of God who worked in the temple of the Lord. Sadly, she became a widow at an early age. Still a young woman, she could've remarried—but from that time on, Anna instead chose to dedicate her life to God and to His temple. She lived and worked there day and night for the next 84 years alongside a priest named Simeon. Her calling from the Lord was to be His prophetess, and God gave her the responsibility to pray and fast for the people of the Lord as well as the ability to speak divine messages to them.

Anna was probably over 100 years old when the events of Luke 2:25-38 occurred, and she had the privilege to see the Messiah, baby Jesus, brought into the temple to be circumcised on his eighth day. It was such an honor for her to see the Savior of the world for herself, she broke out in praise and testimony to all those she encountered in the temple. She was the first person to proclaim to the people of God that the Messiah had been born.

The Bible was clear about Anna's position and purpose in the temple, once more showing how God substantiates the worth of women in the body of Christ. Here we see a beautiful picture in Anna and Simeon of a woman and a man who were not married but worked together in the house of God. They were equally important to God and His purpose for their lives and others. Each had their own gift to contribute to His people. Anna did not have a subservient role. She ministered as a leader in the temple.

If we follow His Word, we will become leaders for Him and a living testimony of His love and holiness so that others will have the opportunity to see how wonderful, loving, and faithful He is to them. We are the only creation that possesses an essence of Him, in that both men and women were given His breath of life and made in His image. As a result, we are His offspring and a true reflection of who He is, designed to show God's image to others. Of course, when Adam and Eve sinned against God by disobeying Him, we inherited a flaw, sin, and His image was tarnished. Thank God that through Jesus and His death on the cross we are now positioned to have the same flawless reflection that Adam and Eve possessed in the beginning.

Priscilla and Aquila were a couple who lived their lives for the Lord, and together they reflected His image to those around them. Introduced in Acts 18, this husband and wife duo were the perfect picture of a marriage relationship that reflected the relationship God has with His people. Whenever they were mentioned in the Bible, their names were always together. Of those six occurrences, Aquila's name was listed first three times and Priscilla's name was first in the other three instances. This indicated the equality in their service to the risen Savior and exhibited their constant oneness. Their lives were sold out to minister to others and show the love of Christ. Priscilla and Aquila taught together, opened their home as a church in Ephesus and in Rome, and aided the apostle Paul in ministry and occupational work as tentmakers in Corinth and Ephesus. They journeyed to various cities teaching and converting others to Christianity, and significantly they taught Apollos, a man well versed in the Old Testament law, and "expounded unto him the way of God more perfectly." (Acts 18:26) Apollos went on to be a renowned preacher and is mentioned in 1 Corinthians 3:6-9 as a co-laborer with Paul in spreading the message of Christ.

It's clear Priscilla was just as important as Aquila in helping and teaching other great men of God. The Lord empowered her and her husband, as dynamic co-laborers for Him, to equally and mightily to get the message of His love out to the world. In *All of the Women of the Bible*, Edith Deen wrote that many honors were heaped upon Priscilla by early Christian writers, including the suggestion that she may even have been the author of the book of Hebrews. To this day, her name appears in Rome on many monuments, in churches, and even in catacombs.

Priscilla and Aquila emulated the oneness God desires to have with us, so much so that He wrapped Himself in flesh to dwell among us as Emmanuel, God with us (Matthew 1:23). They had a beautiful relationship that honored God—and Christ came so that we may have a beautiful relationship with the Father.

When David declared in Psalm 8:9, "Oh Lord, our Lord, how excellent is thy name," I believe he foresaw this glorious plan of restoration from our sins through Jesus. In Psalm 8, David also exulted in how God created everything we need—the stars, moon, sun, planets, plants, animals, oceans, land, and atmosphere—all of it to make provision for His ultimate creation, us! God's provision reminds me of a mother and father preparing for their new baby to come into the world. They make sure all is in place for that child to thrive in life. God did the same for us in creation. He knew our value and He put great thought and care into creating us. That is why He places so much emphasis on us.

Finally, David saw the awesomeness of God and concluded that if He looked upon us as being good, then we must see ourselves that way as well. In his book, *The Search for Significance*, Robert S. McGee states, "God tells us that we are so significant to Him that He always keeps an eye on us. He manages to be so sensitive to our situation that He even keeps track of the hairs on our head. There is obviously nothing more important to God than our welfare."

PSALM 139: THE GOD WHO SEES YOU

"O lord, thou hast searched me, and known me. Thou knowest my downsitting and mine uprising, thou understandest my thought afar off. Thou compassest my path and my lying down, and art acquainted with all my ways. For there is not a word in my tongue, but, lo, O Lord, thou knowest it altogether. Thou hast beset me behind and before, and laid thine hand upon me. Such knowledge is too wonderful for me; it is high, I cannot attain unto it. Whither shall I go from thy spirit? or whither shall I flee from thy presence? If I ascend up into heaven, thou art there: if I make my bed in hell, behold, thou art there. If I take the wings of the morning, and dwell in the uttermost parts of the sea; Even there shall thy hand lead me, and thy right hand shall hold me. If I say, Surely the darkness shall cover me; even the night shall be light about me. Yea, the darkness hideth not from thee; but the night shineth as the day: the darkness and the light are both alike to thee. For thou hast possessed my reins: thou hast covered me in my mother's womb. I will praise thee; for I am fearfully and wonderfully made: marvellous are thy works; and that my soul knoweth right well. My substance was not hid from thee, when I was made in secret, and curiously wrought in the lowest parts of the earth. Thine eyes did see my substance, yet being unperfect; and in thy book all my members were written, which in continuance were fashioned, when as yet there was none of them. How precious also are thy thoughts unto me, O God! how great is the sum of them! If I should count them, they are more in number than the sand: when I awake, I am still with thee. Surely thou wilt slay the wicked, O God: depart from me therefore, ye bloody men. For they speak against thee wickedly, and thine enemies take thy name in vain. Do not I hate them, O Lord, that hate thee? and am not I grieved with those that rise up against thee? I hate them with perfect hatred: I count them mine enemies. Search me, O God, and know my heart: try me, and know my thoughts: And see if there be any wicked way in me, and lead me in the way everlasting." (Psalm 139:1-24)

David began with a confession that God was the ultimate creator who knew everything about him and who was forever present in his life as his provider and protector. Later, David acknowledged that God was concerned about us and our development even when we were in the womb. Just as the Bible in Proverbs 31 alludes to the worth of a virtuous woman as being far above rubies, David realized that we were wonderfully and fearfully made and, therefore, priceless to Him. Then David concluded the Psalm with these memorable words. "Search me, O God, and know my heart; try me, and know my thoughts; And see if there be any wicked way in me, and lead me the way everlasting." David submitted to the Lord full mastership over his life, asking Him to search out anything that was not like God's image so that He could make the changes needed to accurately reflect God in his life.

A woman who allowed the Lord to search her and change her so she could better reflect Him to others is **Mary Magdalene**. Freed by Christ from the mental and spiritual torment of being possessed by seven demons, Mary was not beneath saving. Jesus had compassion on her, and when Mary was delivered, she became a faithful and devoted follower of Jesus. She was grateful and committed to Him out of appreciation for what He did for her, so Mary pledged her life to build His Kingdom. She helped finance the ministry and ministered to Jesus personally. She gave her gifts, talents, and treasure to help His ministry (Luke 8:2-3).

God was concerned about us and our development even when we were in the womb.

While she traveled with Him throughout His ministry, Mary was most notably present at His crucifixion (John 19:25) and resurrection (John 20:1), and she was the first person to see Jesus after He had risen from the dead (Mark 16:9). The scene that morning is one of the greatest in all of Scripture. It was still dark when Mary arrived at the tomb and saw the stone rolled away. Convinced someone had stolen Christ's body, she was distraught and perplexed. Mary was still crying at the tomb when she suddenly saw two angels in white, seated where Jesus' body had been. Moments later, she turned around and saw a man standing before her. She thought he was the gardener. She pleaded, "Sir, if thou have borne him hence, tell me where thou hast laid him, and I will take him away," (John 20:15b)

That's when He said one word—her name—and she knew! It was Jesus! He had risen! Joy swept through her. She wanted to grab Him, hold Him, and kiss His feet out of her love and dedication to Him. Yet "Jesus saith unto her, Touch me not; for I am not yet ascended to my Father: but go to my brethren, and say unto them, I ascend unto my Father, and your Father; and to my God, and your God." Then "Mary Magdalene came and told the disciples that she had seen the Lord, and that he had spoken these things unto her." (John 20:17-18)

What an honor and privilege it must've been to be the first to see Him and then to deliver the incredible news to His disciples. Mary was the first to preach the message of Christ's resurrection! Her story always reminds me of the glorious words of Proverbs 8:17. "I love them that love me; and those that seek me early shall find me."

The Lord constantly loves on us to make us the best we can be. Our full potential comes from being more like our creator, so when there are characteristics in us that do not reflect God, we need to humbly submit and give Him permission to remove them. The Lord understands that we have been flawed, and He is willing to mold and shape us into His image. Then we can once again represent His power, authority, and, most of all, love—so that we can fulfill the ultimate purpose for our life: to bring glory to the Most High God.

Another great woman who brought glory to the Lord in a powerful way was my mother, Vernell, a phenomenal woman of God. She gave her life to the Lord as a child. Her siblings said she was a peculiar child. She loved the nicer things in life and enjoyed cooking, entertaining, and reading magazines about elaborate lifestyles, even though she was a sharecropper's daughter and came from an extremely poor family that worked on a farm. As an adult, my mother was a pastor's wife, speaker and singer, vocational nurse, and an entrepreneur. Growing up, I watched this woman of excellence raise five sons and one daughter, always instilling in us the righteousness of God.

She was strong and boldly courageous. She knew her purpose in God, and she carried it out well. She possessed the gift of making people feel important and worthy of love. She had her own home ministry that helped women. I remember there was always someone living with us as she helped them get back on their feet. One time, my mother moved a female member of our church into her guest room while the woman suffered through migraine headaches. My mother served her day and night, making her food, helping her get dressed, covering the windows with sheets so the sunlight couldn't get in to aggravate her headaches, and taking her to the doctor—never once asking for anything in return. The woman stayed with us for several weeks until she was able to go home and take care of herself.

My mother repeatedly told me, "The higher you go in ministry, Elaine, the more of a servant you are." She taught our church's women's Bible study in her home every Tuesday night. It was attended by ladies of all ages, and she showed us how to be women of God, care for our children, love our husbands, and keep up our homes. I recall one of her many impressionable sayings: "A woman can waste more with a teaspoon than a man can bring in with a shovel," referring to how frugal and wise we needed to be with the money our husbands brought home to the family. "Just because it is on sale," she added, "does not mean you need to buy it," noting that we should only purchase those things truly needed for our families.

One of the many practical lessons she taught us concerned clothing. My mother looked fantastic in what she wore and always chose the best outfits. "You buy dresses for twenty dollars, but then you wash and tear," she would say of how the washing process quickly took a toll on cheap clothes. "So, save your money and buy a nice piece of clothing that will last for years. After you buy four dresses at twenty dollars, you could have bought one dress for fifty that you will still be wearing." That spoke to her earlier saying about throwing away the $30 difference with a teaspoon. Another nugget of wisdom she told others was, "It's not how you get to

Chicago, ladies, as long as you get there." She meant that we should do whatever is necessary to get the things we want by humbling ourselves and learning not to lean on our own understanding, but instead acknowledge God and let Him direct our paths (Proverbs 3:5-6). We are to be satisfied with how God imparts His plan for us. It may not be the way we envisioned it to be, but it's the best way for us and our circumstances. My mother taught practical Christian living. If we put God first, everything else was going to work out.

During the holidays, my mother had young women bring ingredients for their holiday dinners to our home, and then she helped them cook their Thanksgiving, Christmas, or Easter meals. As she had with me, she taught them how to set the table and gave them advice on how to host dinners for their family and friends. Her ministry to others extended beyond the church. She once gave herself to another young woman going through a devastating divorce from her husband who was a minister. She opened our home to her to just talk, and she was there for her. "The toughest time is night because that is when you stop doing things," Vernell told her, so she called the young woman every night, sometimes talking into the wee hours of the morning. My mother counseled other women who were not Christians, and they eventually became believers in Jesus through her loving witness. Another woman, who was a prostitute, came to our house for food and to rest and talk, and my mother never made a differentiation between her and women who were in the church. That woman ultimately became a Christian, later opened a home to minister to mentally disabled men, and became one of the most faithful members of our church.

My mother never judged others. She simply accepted them

You are important to God—and not limited to one purpose in life.

just as they were. However, she always encouraged them to not *stay* where they were but to grow and mature. Her entrepreneurial bent manifested itself when she placed her famous sweet potato pies on the market. A major grocery chain picked them up and started selling them in the frozen food section. Her business was just about to take off when my oldest brother became ill with cancer, yet she stopped all pie production to take him into her home and care for him until he died.

There are hundreds, if not thousands, of women who carry the teachings of Sister Vernell Jones. She had a nontraditional way of reaching people of any economic status, race, education, or religious affiliation, but she remained powerful in her walk with the Lord and in loving others. I used to tell her we had two churches, the one downtown and the one in her home, both building the Kingdom of God.

Today, I still know I was right.

Daughter of the King, you are important to God—and not limited to one purpose in life. God has many things in store for you to do, but you must be diligent in examining the gifts the Lord has planted within you. You have so much to offer, and if you walk in His purposes for you, the message of His love for the world will be proclaimed through you! You need to be passionate about His Word, and as you are, the affirmation of His love for you will inspire you to share His love with others.

Your love for God your Father will put this expression of love into action. You may not even have to mention the name of Jesus to show it. My mother used to say, "Don't be so heavenly righteous until your no earthly good," meaning that you do not have to push God on others. Your sincere actions will make an impact on someone's life because it is the God *within* you that people will see and experience.

In addition, don't look for anything in return when showing the love of God to others. You don't have to be out front as you carry forth His purposes, but that doesn't mean you are any less important to Him. Whatever the Lord uses you to do is vital to you and to the person you touch for Him. Priscilla and her husband, Aquila, opened their home, taught scholars the words of God, and brought many converts to the church. Mary Magdalene helped finance Jesus' ministry. Anna chose to dedicate her life to the Lord by working in the temple. My life was changed in a miraculous way to touch the lives of women and children. My mother used practical everyday living to exhibit the love of God and, in turn, had opportunities to share His Word.

Remember, it's not how you get to Chicago as long as you get there. You do not have to be like everyone else. *Be you!* The Lord will use you in His own way. It is likely He will use you in unique ways no one else could've done. Know what God has placed in you to do—and then do it to the best of your ability and with great passion.

Chapter 6

"Favour is deceitful, and beauty is vain:
but a woman that feareth the Lord, she shall be praised."
(Proverbs 31:30)

Thus far, we have looked at the stories of some incredible women in the Bible—Mary, Jochebed, Deborah, Rahab, Tabitha (Dorcas), the Woman at the Well, Elizabeth, Rebekah, the "Sinful" Woman, Esther, Priscilla (with her husband Aquila), and Mary Magdalene—all incredible, but also all well-recognized women from Scripture. Yet there are other significant women, particularly in the Old Testament, who are not as well-known but whose stories are inspiring and more than worthy of declaration.

As we meet these magnificent women, allow your heart to receive what God wants to speak to you—and do through you—because of how precious and important you are to Him.

A BLESSING: THE SHUNAMMITE WOMAN

We do not know the name of our next Old Testament woman of substance, but she has a notably beautiful story. A prominent Jewish woman of influence and wealth, we first meet her in 2 Kings 4, living in Shunem and married to an older man. What stands out about this woman is her faith and that she was giving and hospitable, especially to those traveling through her city. She used her substance to look for opportunities to help. This was especially true when it came to the "man of God," Elisha the prophet.

As she looked and saw Elisha walking by her home, she called out to him to stop, rest from his journey, and have dinner with her and her husband. She saw a need and sought to meet the need immediately. Her status and affluence did not deter her from helping others; in fact, it inspired her to do so. Her attitude was one of servitude, not of someone who wanted to be served herself. She wanted to be a blessing instead of looking to be blessed. Women of substance should always seek to be a blessing to those around them, no matter their financial, emotional, or spiritual state. We are to understand that blessing awaits those who are a blessing to others.

In the case of the Shunammite woman, her heart was pure, with no ulterior motive in her generosity. The Bible says it is better to give than to receive (Acts 20:35), meaning if you have it to give, you are already blessed, so the blessing is in the giving, not the receiving. In Luke 6:38, Jesus said, "Give, and it shall be given unto you; good measure, pressed down, and shaken together, and running over, shall men give into your bosom. For with the same measure that ye mete withal it shall be measured to you again." Here, Christ shared with the multitude a principle of character and of how we should live as His followers: the blessing is all in the giving! The Shunammite woman knew this. She had a giving heart—and that applies to our service to God as well. We must give Him everything. We should not always ask for things, but our first thought should be to ask God, "What can I give to you? How can I be a blessing to you and your Kingdom, Lord?" A woman of substance will show God's character by giving back to Him and then giving to others. After all, "For God so loved the world, that he gave…" (John 3:16) Following the example of the Shunammite woman, give—of yourself, your substance, and your time, flowing from a loving and cheerful heart with no expectation of return. That is what it means to "love the Lord thy God with all thy heart, and with all thy soul, and with all thy mind." (Matthew 22:37)

Since the Shunammite woman was so magnanimous in her giving, Elisha felt comfortable enough with her that he made it a point to go by her house whenever he passed through her city. Not only did she provide for him, but she also looked beyond the immediate need and focused on a more permanent way to make him welcome during his visits. She said to her husband,

> "Let us make a little chamber, I pray thee, on the wall; and let us set for him there a bed, and a table, and a stool, and a candlestick: and it shall be, when he cometh to us, that he shall turn in thither." (2 Kings 4:10)

Her heart and mind were set on what *more* she could do for the man of God who journeyed many miles to minister to other people.

Ask yourself, "When was the last time I was a blessing to the man or woman of God in my life? What have I done to make his or her appointment easier?" They're challenging questions. We often look to bless those who are needy or less fortunate, which is good—but we should always think about the needs of those who are responsible for our spiritual growth as well. Blessing them is a double blessing for you. Not only will you be blessed spiritually, but you will be blessed personally, too, because serving the man or woman of God is an act of giving to the Lord.

So, the Shunammite woman saw that Elisha not only needed food and rest, but a place to lay his head where he could read the Torah and get the extended refreshment he needed. She consulted with her husband to build a special room for the man of God, and she was meticulously detailed about what the room should include. Once her husband agreed with her idea, she executed the plan to create the room. This was beyond the call of duty to serve another—and she was happy to do it.

The next time Elisha visited her home, she presented the new space to him. He was so impressed with her hospitality that he wanted to bless her in return. He asked if there was anything he could do for her. Amazingly, she wanted nothing in return for her generosity, even when Elisha insisted on doing something for her. Her response was iconic. She said, "I dwell among mine own people." (2 Kings 4:13) She was satisfied to simply live among her Jewish brothers and sisters. Her family had everything they needed. She wanted nothing more.

But she did have a deep, personal need—one that wasn't revealed until Elisha pressed his servant, Gehazi, for the information: the Shunammite woman had no children, and it was considered a dishonor in biblical times for a woman to be childless.

Once the man of God realized this, he gave her an incredible promise: within a year she was going to have a child. She couldn't believe it. "Nay, my lord, thou man of God, do not lie unto thine handmaid." (2 Kings 4:16) Her response wasn't disrespectful. She simply felt it was close to impossible and didn't want Elisha to fool her. Her husband was old, and she did not think she could conceive.

Yet she did! Exactly as the man of God said, she conceived and gave birth to a son—and the Shunammite woman delighted herself in the Lord her God who gave her the desire of her heart (Psalms 37:4). She was happy to help the man of God, and the Lord was happy to give her a son.

While we will receive blessings from God, we will also encounter tragedies in life. Such was the case for the Shunammite woman. Several years later, perhaps a decade or so, her boy went out among the reapers with his father in the heat of the day and suddenly became ill. The father had the son taken to his mother. She held him until noon, and then he died. Devastated, the woman went to her husband and asked if she could have a donkey to go to Elisha.

This prominent, influential woman did not disregard her husband. She sought him with her decisions. A woman of substance will always respect her husband and honor his position in the family in every situation.

Interestingly, though, the Shunammite woman did not tell her husband that their son had died, likely to spare him the grief. Instead, as she prepared to leave, she told him, "It shall be well." (2 Kings 4:23) Her faith in God—and in the man of God—assured her that everything was going to be alright. Her strength was phenomenal. She cared for her son until he died in her arms, carried him to the chamber designated for Elisha, then carried the death of her only child by herself so as not to worry her husband. Next, she immediately traveled several miles to go to the man of God, including a climb up Mount Carmel to get to Elisha and then traveled back to her home. She did all of those things in one day, all while holding herself together physically and emotionally. What an example of great strength and of a woman of substance!

Her faith moved her to go to the man of God—and it is your faith in God that will move you to your miracle. Your faith will sustain you until His divine plan comes to fruition in your life!

Once the Shunammite woman arrived, she was met by Gehazi. When he tried to find out what she needed, she told him "It is well." There it is again! I believe it was her way of encouraging her own faith in the powerful God she served. She knew all was well. When we are faced with hard, adverse situations, may our resolve allow us to say, as she did, "It is well!" Why? Because no matter what *it* is, "it" covers it all. No matter how severe or significant it may be, it is well because of our Savior. We know Christ is the head of our lives and has all power in Heaven and Earth. We can say that because our resolve is in our faith in what He can do!

Determined to see Elisha,

"when she came to the man of God to the hill, she caught him by the feet: but Gehazi came near to thrust her away. And the man of God said, Let her alone; for her soul is vexed within her: and the Lord hath hid it from me, and hath not told me." (2 Kings 4:27)

I can see her not even looking at Gehazi while never breaking her stride to get to Elisha, then falling at his feet and beginning to weep, allowing all of her grief and sorrow to flow. Her emotions were not an expression of doubt, but of a broken heart. It is always okay to cry out to the Lord. He exhorts us to cast all our cares on Him, for He cares for us (1 Peter 5:7). He hears the cries of His people.

When we face devastating circumstances, we must go determinedly and directly to our source of help, God—and seeking out the man or woman of God in our lives can also be helpful. As Matthew 18:19-20 tells us, "If two of you shall agree on earth as touching anything that they shall ask, it shall be done for them of my Father which is in heaven. For where two or three are gathered together in my name, there am I in the midst of them." Seek someone who is strong in faith and has a constant relationship with the Lord when you need to pray for something specific. That is the person who can help you maintain your faith.

Seeing and knowing the woman's need, Elisha ordered Gehazi to go on ahead, take his staff, and place it on the boy while Elisha followed behind. When Elisha arrived, the boy remained dead, but Elisha,

"went up, and lay upon the child, and put his mouth upon his mouth, and his eyes upon his eyes, and his hands upon his hands: and stretched himself upon the child; and the flesh of the child waxed warm. Then he returned, and walked in the house to and fro; and went up, and stretched himself upon him: and the child sneezed seven times, and the child opened his eyes. And he called Gehazi, and said, Call this Shunammite. So he called her. And when she was come in unto him, he said, Take up thy son." (2 Kings 4:34-36)

The boy was resurrected and given back to his mother and father!

The next time we meet the Shunammite woman is in 2 Kings 8:1-6. Elisha must have continued staying at her home whenever he traveled because he then told her that she should leave because of a seven-year famine coming to her town and the surrounding area. Predictably, she and her son followed the instructions of the man of God (her husband was not mentioned here, likely because he was deceased) and moved to the land of the Philistines for seven years.

The famine came and passed, but because she had been away for so long, others had taken possession of her house and land. With characteristic strength and boldness, the woman entered the palace to get help from the king—at the same exact moment the king was asking Gehazi about Elisha and the miracles he performed. Isn't God's providence incredible? Because of this "coincidence," she was present to attest to Elisha's miracles to the king, and as a result the king ordered that everything she had lost be restored to her! God used the Shunammite woman once more to bless the man of God, and in return, she was blessed to get all of her property back.

The Lord will give you opportunities to be a blessing to others.

The Lord will give you opportunities to be a blessing to others and will then bless you in response. When God calls you, be like the Shunammite woman. Be generous, be humble, be obedient— and then be amazed at what God does for you, to His glory!

WISE PEACEMAKER: ABIGAIL

Our next Old Testament woman of substance is only mentioned a handful of times in the Bible, but the story most associated with her shows her quality, character, and wisdom. First introduced in Scripture in 1 Samuel 25, we are told Abigail was intelligent, beautiful, and a woman who feared God—but she was married to a brutal fool named Nabal. Nabal descended from the house of Caleb, the Israelite spy who scouted out the Promised Land with Joshua and who was a great man of God. Unfortunately, Nabal did not inherit any of Caleb's attributes. Nabal was described as cruel, evil, and thoughtless. If Abigail was so wise, you might wonder, why was she married to such a man? Remember, in biblical times women did not have a say in who they wed. Marriages were arranged, a socially acceptable practice during that time that still happens today in other cultures.

Abigail lived in a troubled relationship and an unhappy home, but she made the best of it because she was able to find peace through her God. Many women find themselves in troubled marriages like Abigail's, and she provided a perfect example of how to deal wisely with an alcoholic, brutal, and verbal abuser of a husband. In her case, she had no recourse but to stay and trust God. In biblical times, women didn't have any way of taking care of themselves financially. In fact, women generally didn't have any value in the culture, and in most cases had to be married in order to survive. But in today's society, if you are currently in a physically abusive relationship, you need to get out and get help. Go to your church pastor or first lady or a trusted family member. Call a women's abuse hotline, the police, or a good friend. God can do anything in your marriage and for you and your husband, but both parties have to be willing to work on themselves and the relationship. A woman of substance must go to God and depend on His guidance, trusting Him and His instruction, and then do exactly what He tells her to do.

Early in my marriage, my husband and I were not getting along. I felt he was being mean and distant. He rarely had much to say to me, and every time I tried to talk to him, he closed up even more. At first, I decided to respond to my husband in the same way. I treated him as if he wasn't there. But weeks went on, and nothing was resolved. In frustration and despair, I went to God in my secret place and cried out to Him for guidance. When I finished praying, the Holy Spirit instructed me to cook dinner and set a nice table—not just any dinner, but a full Sunday dinner on a Thursday night: fried chicken, cabbage, cornbread, rice, and gravy. I created a beautiful table complete with candles and flowers. Through all of the preparation, I wept because I felt I was having to humble myself while my husband was the one guilty of wrongdoing. I didn't think it was fair for me to do something nice for someone who was not being nice to me.

At one point a friend called. "What are you doing?" she asked.

"I'm cooking a big meal for me and my husband," I responded, trying to hold back my tears.

"Why are you doing all of that tonight?" She sounded surprised, almost exasperated with me.

I sobbed. "Because God told me to."

She quickly ended the call. She didn't know what to think. In a way, neither did I.

When my husband came home, he walked right past the candlelit table—and right past me—straight to the bedroom, without saying a word. I began setting out the food. I felt so foolish. "Why did I do all of this?" I asked God quietly. "He didn't even stop to eat." Almost 30 minutes later, he finally came, sat down at the table, and started eating. Again, he didn't speak and neither did I. When he was done, he got up, went into the family room, and turned on the television.

I was devastated. I just sat there, staring down at the half-eaten food still on my plate, consumed by a hurt in my heart that was impossible to explain. Eventually, I got up, cleared the table, and started washing the dishes. Tears streamed down my face. All I had done was for nothing.

I was cleaning one of the final pans when I heard my husband walk into the kitchen.

"Elaine—I'm sorry," he began, and then he told me what he was feeling inside and why he had become so distant. All these years later, I don't remember the specific issues as much as I do the amazement I felt as I saw the promise of God fulfilled in my marriage. I had not said a word. I had simply obeyed the voice of the Lord. Even when I questioned Him, it was through my silence and my obedience that the Lord had the opportunity to soften my husband's heart. That night, God began to fortify our marriage.

Every woman's situation is unique, and God may instruct you to do something different. But remain obedient to the Lord and humble before Him and your husband—and the Lord will work on him. When I teach women, I use the phrase "shut it down" to support the idea of remaining silent and keeping the joy of the Lord as your strength. No matter how bad it is, your marriage does not have to end in divorce. God can reconcile and restore your relationship as you remain faithful to do what is right in His sight. In her book, *The Power of a Praying Wife*, Stormie Omartian says the breakthrough comes by "laying down all claim on power in and of yourself, and relying on God's power to transform you, your husband, your circumstance, and your marriage … It is a gentle tool of restoration appropriated through the prayers of a wife who longs to do right more than to be right and to give life more than get even."

In her situation, Abigail existed mentally and emotionally outside of her current circumstances, relying on the Lord as her confidant and living with joy, true to the meaning of her name. Even in her decidedly bad situation, Abigail did not gossip, nor was she angry, bitter, and mean. Instead, she put her energy into others, using her talents for good and showing kindness to the servants and everyone else around her. Yet despite her goodness, Nabal's ignorance and arrogance brought trouble that affected the lives of all those in their household.

While David and his army of 600 men were running from Saul, they met Nabal's shepherds in the wilderness, became allies with them, and provided for their protection. Eventually, David and his men needed food from Nabal and assumed he was going to honor the request, as proper hospitality and respect dictated. David sent 10 of his men to Nabal with specific instructions for what to say.

> "And thus you shall greet him: 'Peace be to you, and peace be to your house, and peace be to all that you have. I hear that you have shearers. Now your shepherds have been with us, and we did them no harm, and they missed nothing all the time they were in Carmel. Ask your young men, and they will tell you. Therefore let my young men find favor in your eyes, for we come on a feast day. Please give whatever you have at hand to your servants and to your son David." (1 Samuel 25:6-8, ESV)

But Nabal, in a drunken stupor, told the young men he owed nothing to the no name rogue. "Who is David? Who is the son of Jesse?" he sarcastically quipped. "There are many servants these days who are breaking away from their masters." (1 Samuel 25:10) When David was told Nabal's response, he became furious and prepared his men for battle. He was so angry, he planned to kill everyone in Nabal's household.

When Nabal's servants got wind of this, they did something quite interesting. Instead of going to Nabal himself, they went straight to Abigail. They had great confidence in her ability to resolve this life-threatening danger—and she immediately went into action.

> "Then Abigail made haste and took two hundred loaves and two skins of wine and five sheep already prepared and five seahs of parched grain and a hundred clusters of raisins and two hundred cakes of figs, and laid them on donkeys. And she said to her young men, 'Go on before me; behold, I come after you.' But she did not tell her husband Nabal." (1 Samuel 25:18-19, ESV)

Abigail responded to David's request for food—and then some. Even more, she knew she had to get everything to him before he came into town. If she waited, she knew it would be too late. Showing incredible wisdom, Abigail led a small caravan out to meet David and his men to serve him, reason with him, and extinguish his anger. She knew Nabal had been malicious with his speech and had insulted David to the point of attack.

God surely had guided her on what to do and how to handle this particular situation. Our Lord is always ready and willing to guide us through every challenge or attack we encounter. James 1:5 tells us, "If any of you lacks wisdom, let him ask God, who gives generously to all without reproach, and it will be given him." (ESV) Wisdom comes from God, and He not only wants us to have it, but He gives it freely.

Our Lord is always ready and willing to guide us through every challenge.

Clearly, Abigail had received much wisdom from the Lord. What bravery it must've taken for her to go out and meet David and his men! She knew they were coming to kill her entire household, yet she approached David—not with bold bravado, but in humble reverence. She bowed down at David's feet, giving him the respect that her husband Nabal witlessly refused to give, and only afterward did she ask for permission to speak. Abigail treated David as the king he'd someday become.

Next, she sought to defuse David's wrath by openly admitting that her husband was as foolish as his name suggested. She also said that if she had known his men were there, the insult would never have happened, and she would've honored his request for food and help. Then Abigail tapped David's love for God and what the Lord had revealed to him about his destiny. How else could she have known about this except by God's revelation and wisdom? She went directly to the core of David's heart. She reminded him of his future and how God had promised him a great dynasty; therefore, he should not waste his time with a fool such as her husband because David was greater than that—and had greatness ahead of him. She believed it, too, because she closed her plea by asking him to remember her kindness when he came into his kingship.

God has placed greatness in all of us. It may not be on a big public platform. It may be in the privacy of your home or workplace. But whatever and wherever it is, in order to honor the greatness that He has given us, and because we have been called by God into His family, we cannot engage in foolishness or become involved with foolish people.

In the early 1990s, when I was working at the Federal Deposit Insurance Corporation, Madonna put out a book of nude photographs—and one of my coworkers, whose desk was right in front of mine, brought the book into the office. Everybody swarmed to his cubicle, and I heard the "oohs" and "ahhs" of those taking a peek. After a couple of minutes, I thought, *I'll get up and take a look, too, just to see what all the hoopla is about.*

Instantly, the Holy Spirit said, "No. Do not engage."

I stayed seated, and moments later someone looked over and said, "Elaine, you've got to see this."

"No," I said. "That's not for me."

Then the Holy Spirit whispered to my heart, "It would've compromised your witness for me if you would've engaged." We've got to be careful to avoid foolishness that could hinder or undermine God's greatness in our lives. We're bigger than that, and He is far more important.

For David to engage in a foolish revenge-driven battle against Nabal's household would have been his demise. Yet Abigail surely said all the right things to David that fateful day—because he calmed down and listened to her. He accepted her provision and blessed her discretion. Through her prudent, courageous response, Abigail saved the lives of thousands of people. Even more, God took care of Abigail as she dealt with two hot-tempered men, one who was a fool and the other who was facing turmoil. The Lord used Abigail to save David from having blood on his hands—and then proceeded to save Abigail, too, in a most unexpected way.

> "Abigail came to Nabal, and behold, he was holding a feast in his house, like the feast of a king. And Nabal's heart was merry within him, for he was very drunk. So she told him nothing at all until the morning light. In the morning, when the wine had gone out of Nabal, his wife told him these things, and his heart died within him, and he became as a stone. And about ten days later the Lord struck Nabal, and he died. When David heard that Nabal was dead, he said, 'Blessed be the Lord who has avenged the insult I received at the hand of Nabal, and has kept back his servant from wrongdoing. The Lord has returned the evil of Nabal on his own head.' Then David sent and spoke to Abigail, to take her as his wife. When the servants of David

came to Abigail at Carmel, they said to her, 'David has sent us to you to take you to him as his wife.' And she rose and bowed with her face to the ground and said, 'Behold, your handmaid is a servant to wash the feet of the servants of my lord.' And Abigail hurried and rose and mounted a donkey, and her five young women attended her. She followed the messengers of David and became his wife." (1 Samuel 25:36-42, ESV)

SUBMISSIVE COURAGE: SARAI (SARAH)

From Sarai to Sarah, the name God gave to her later, she was the mother of the Hebrew nation, God's chosen people who received His covenant promise of love and salvation. Sarai was from the country of Ur of the Chaldeans. She was married to her half-brother Abram (later Abraham), and she was so beautiful that men would kill to have her (Genesis 12:11-12). Sarai was a woman who believed in God—and in her husband. She was a woman of great strength and influence, so much so that while the Lord had chosen Abram to be the father of His covenant nation, He did not exclude Sarai and honored her role as mother of the people. Many women believe that because God has placed a calling on their husband's life, they do not have a calling themselves—but that is not true. God has placed you in ministry together. You have various gifts that should enhance your husband's calling, and vice versa. The two of you work in unison to build His Kingdom.

Abram was told by God to leave his country to go to a place that He would show him. Abram obeyed the Lord, but what is most significant is that Sarai followed without a fight. She didn't know where she was going, but she trusted her husband and his faith in God. Along the journey, they were confronted by a severe famine that forced them to travel into Egypt. Before entering that land, Abram came up with a scheme to save his life.

"He said to Sarai his wife, 'I know that you are a woman beautiful in appearance, and when the Egyptians see you, they will say, "This is his wife." Then they will kill me, but they will let you live. Say you are my sister, that it may go well with me because of you, and that my life may be spared for your sake.' When Abram entered Egypt, the Egyptians saw that the woman was very beautiful. And when the princes of Pharaoh saw her, they praised her to Pharaoh. And the woman was taken into Pharaoh's house. And for her sake he dealt well with Abram; and he had sheep, oxen, male donkeys, male servants, female servants, female donkeys, and camels." (Genesis 12:11-16, ESV)

Here we see Sarai's total submission and courage. She did not try to save her own honor; instead, she went along with Abram's idea, knowing it would make her one of the Pharaoh's concubines. Abram did not care about Sarai's well-being or what could happen to her. He thought only of himself. But look at God and His divine provision.

"But the Lord afflicted Pharaoh and his house with great plagues because of Sarai, Abram's wife. So Pharaoh called Abram and said, 'What is this you have done to me? Why did you not tell me that she was your wife? Why did you say, "She is my sister," so that I took her for my wife? Now then, here is your wife; take her, and go.' And Pharaoh gave men orders concerning him, and they sent him away with his wife and all that he had." (Genesis 12:17-20, ESV)

Before the Pharaoh could violate Sarai, God placed a curse on the entire palace—bringing Pharaoh to the conclusion that there was something more to Sarai than he had been told. Again, notice

Sarai's strength and character. Even though she had been placed in harm's way by her husband, she did not tell the Pharaoh that she was Abram's wife. Though Abram was not protecting Sarai, God was. Sarai's name means princess, or one in command, and God, the King, was obligated to protect His daughter—just as He is committed to protect *you* as His daughter.

I am enamored with the part of the wedding ceremony where the minister asks, "Who gives this woman to be married to this man?" I see that moment as a transfer of the bride from the father's protection and provision to that of the husband. Furthermore, I see God transferring to the husband the responsibility to love and protect his wife as He does for her as His daughter. This is why Ephesians 5:25-26 says, "Husbands, love your wives, as Christ loved the church and gave himself up for her" (ESV), or, as The Message renders it, "Husbands, go all out in your love for your wives, exactly as Christ did for the church."

> *The Lord will always love, defend, and protect women who call on Him.*

Love, protection, and provision become the husband's role, but God continues to cover His daughters when husband's fail in their responsibility, as Abram did with Sarai. She trusted in God and waited for Him to rescue her. The Lord will always love, defend, and protect women who call on Him. Not only did the Pharaoh release her unharmed, but because of her, Abram became wealthy, being sent away with all he had acquired from the Pharaoh.

Proverbs 18:22 declares, "He who finds a wife finds a good thing and obtains favor from the Lord." (ESV) This story from Sarai's life shows this scripture in action. God's favor is on display throughout, and not only is it clear that Abram had a good wife, but he obtained so much because she was a woman of God. Sarai brought God's favor to her husband. It is so important for every man to understand this—as it is equally vital for every woman to live out her life as a devout woman of God.

Of course, Sarai had both the Lord's favor and His provision in addition to being beautiful and married to a man of God—but there was one thing she lacked. She could not have children. Sarai knew that God had promised that her and Abram would be parents, but she was long past child-bearing age and had become impatient as she dealt with the agony of being barren. So, as told in Genesis 16, Sarai decided to help God out. She sought to fulfill His promise in her own way.

We must remain steadfast and immovable when we are waiting on the Lord, walking by faith and not wavering, no matter what it looks like. If God promises something, He will deliver. When we doubt God and try to intervene on our own, we get in the way of His miracle. We won't stop it, but our interference can cause more problems for us in the future. As women, we naturally want to fix things, yet sometimes fear, or even panic, can rise up in our souls as we seek to address the problem. That's when we need to remember that God have given us all the ability that we need to be fixers—but we have to be careful not to go forward without His direction. In fact, there will be times when God convicts us to step back and let Him take care of the problem. That's hard to hear, but as His daughters we must trust in our Father when He directs us to "let go and let God."

Sarai, though, sought to fix her problem on her own and came up with a simple plan: Abram could have sex with her maidservant, Hagar, then Sarai would raise that child as if it were her own. But after she conceived, we are told Hagar looked upon Sarai with contempt. Whether or not this was actually true, or just what Sarai believed, is unknown. It may have been that Hagar did indeed see Sarai as less significant because she was carrying Abram's child when Sarai could not. At any rate, the situation prompted Sarai to complain to her husband.

"Sarai said to Abram, 'May the wrong done to me be on you! I gave my servant to your embrace, and when she saw that she had conceived, she looked on me with contempt. May the Lord judge between you and me!' But Abram said to Sarai, 'Behold, your servant is in your power; do to her as you please.'" (Genesis 16:5-6, ESV)

Here were two women, living in the same house with one husband, both feeling they were important in their own right—Sarai being both the official wife and Hagar's mistress, and Hagar being servant but also the mother of Abram's seed. Yet Sarai's attitude was that Hagar was the problem even though it was all her idea in the first place. As a result, Sarai "dealt harshly" with Hagar to the point that Hagar ran away (Genesis 16:6).

Sometimes we can create situations for ourselves that turn out to be a huge problem and then blame someone else rather than take responsibility for our own actions. As women of substance, God wants us to take ownership of how we think and what we do. If we don't, we can end up causing ourselves and others a great deal of harm. In this story, Sarai abused Hagar and caused her to flee into the harsh wilderness while she was pregnant. Yet here comes God once more, despite Sarai's error. Look at what happened to Hagar.

"The angel of the Lord found her by a spring of water in the wilderness, the spring on the way to Shur. And he said, 'Hagar, servant of Sarai, where have you come from and where are you going?' She said, 'I am fleeing from my mistress Sarai.' The angel of the Lord said to her, 'Return to your mistress and submit to her.' The angel of the Lord also said to her, 'I will surely multiply your offspring so that they cannot be numbered for multitude.'" (Genesis 16:7-10, ESV)

Incredible! Hagar, the lowly Egyptian servant, likely acquired by Sarai when Abram lied to the Pharaoh, had an encounter with the living God! She had already seen the power of God. After all, she was with Sarai when He sent the plague to Pharaoh's palace on Sarai's behalf. She saw Abram left Egypt with more than he had when he arrived. She also watched Abram's sincere devotion to the Lord when he defeated the kings of many nations with 318 men to save his nephew Lot (Genesis 14:1-16) and then was blessed by the King of Salem after he defeated his enemies (Genesis 14:17-20). All of this had undoubtedly been a blessing for Hagar to experience—but this moment in the wilderness was something else entirely. She personally *saw* that God was real, did speak, and could be trusted in her time of trouble. No wonder Hagar made this declaration: "So she called the name of the Lord who spoke to her, 'You are a God of seeing,' for she said, 'Truly here I have seen him who looks after me.' Therefore the well was called Beer-lahai-roi." (Genesis 16:13-14, ESV)

Through the presence, witness, and even mistakes of Abram and Sarai, Hagar got to know the true God for herself. She was so overjoyed that the same God that talked to, protected, and blessed them was now protecting and talking to her! Even more, God gave her a child, who was to be named Ishmael, a promise similar to the one given to Abram and Sarai, saying that his offspring would be a great multitude. God saw Hagar's heart and showed His compassion to her—and He will do the same for you, no matter your culture, gender, economic status, or educational level. God loves us all, and whoever calls on the name of the Lord shall be saved. If you want to know God and are sincere in your heart about it, He will reveal Himself to you.

Likewise, the witness of your life will impact the lives of others, especially those who do not believe the same as you do. In Egypt, Hagar surely served multiple gods, but her exposure to the one true God through Abram and Sarai influenced her life. By the time she was cast out, Hagar had developed her own faith in God. It was *Him* she called out to in the wilderness. Like Sarai did with Hagar, we can sometimes scorn unbelievers or be arrogant about our beliefs without even knowing it. But when we accept those who do not believe as we do with love and respect, God is able to use our lives to make Himself real to them. The way we walk and talk will have a great impact on the non-believer's life.

So, Hagar trusted in and followed God's instruction. She went back to Abram and Sarai for Ishmael's birth, no matter how hard it was for her to return to the woman who had mistreated her. Sometimes the Lord will tell you to do something similarly difficult, but strive to do as He directs, knowing it is for your good. Through it all, He will protect you and keep you if you obey and do not go outside the Word of God.

In the end, Sarai wasn't perfect. She had flaws. But she was noted in Scripture for her submissive faith (Hebrews 11:11, 1 Peter 3:6) and was a strong and devout woman of God who trusted in and submitted to Him and to her own husband with respect and honor. In 1 Peter 3:4-6, we are called Sarah's daughters as we do good in His sight and let go of our fear. Seek God and trust in His Word for all of your life decisions. You will have a better and greater outcome if you do it God's way instead of your own—and He will be pleased with you. Do not allow your mistakes to define who you are, because God does not see you by your mistakes, but by who He has ordained you to become. We will make some wrong decisions out of anxiety and distrust, but we must thank God for His favor and provision even when we are afraid or in doubt.

Chapter 7

"The Spirit of the Lord is upon me, because he hath
anointed me to preach the gospel to the poor; he hath sent
me to heal the brokenhearted, to preach deliverance
to the captives, and recovering of sight to the blind,
to set at liberty them that are bruised."
(Luke 4:18)

Now that we have been blessed by the Shunammite woman,
Abigail, and Sarai (along with Hagar) from the pages of the
Old Testament, let's turn to the New Testament for more amazing stories of significant women—some of whom, perhaps, you've never met in your prior reading of Scripture.

The first story is particularly worthy of your attention, for it tells of the love and compassion God has for His daughters and declares anew how important you are to Him.

AN UNASKED-FOR MIRACLE:
THE WIDOW OF NAIN

In Luke 7:11-16, we meet a woman in utter despair. Not only is she grieving the loss of her only son and is in the process of burying him, but she has no husband and is, therefore, facing the loss of her home, of any hope of income, and of her dignity. In fact, it's likely the only future she could see for herself was as a beggar on the street. A woman without a man in biblical times was destitute. It's hard to imagine the uncertainty she must've felt as a widow whose son was now dead. Her mind raced from deep sorrow to paralyzing fear as she walked with the crowd of people, most of the people in the town of Nain, to lay her child to rest. She had once before walked this procession with her husband's body—and now this? From whom could she possibly hope to receive comfort or help?

Here comes Jesus, who had just arrived in the tiny settlement after entering Capernaum the day before.

> "And when the Lord saw her, he had compassion on her, and said unto her, Weep not." (Luke 7:13)

I can see the Lord locking His eyes on the widow mother as He saw her hurt and desperation. He discerned the condition of her heart and immediately wanted to aid her—and that's where the compassion comes in. She did not even have to ask for His intervention. Surely, she was too grief-stricken to ask, and why would she seek His help anyway? Her son was about to be buried. It was way too late for anyone to change anything. Remember, Jesus had yet to raise a person from the dead. She could not have known He was capable of such a miracle, even if she had heard of the other wonders He had performed. Jesus then said to her, "Weep not." With that simple exhortation, He proclaimed, "I have the answer for your sorrow. I see your pain. I know what you're facing."

In Exodus 22:22-24, God commanded the Hebrew people to take care of the widows and orphans among them. The Lord is very serious and specific with us about our responsibility toward the vulnerable, and in this story, Christ modeled how we should feel about those who are less fortunate. He also displayed His love for us, in that even when we sometimes do not ask for His help, He still knows our hearts and will meet our needs.

Jesus lovingly and boldly acted on the widow's behalf.

"And he came and touched the bier: and they that bare him stood still. And he said, Young man, I say unto thee, Arise." (Luke 7:14)

According to Hebrew law, no rabbi could touch a dead body or the bier that bore it. But Christ looked beyond tradition to perform a miracle! His actions communicated that a woman's need was important enough to stop a funeral procession, touch a bier, and save a person from despair. By doing all of that, He substantiated women. That's in alignment with how He substantiated the Gentiles the day before when He helped a centurion soldier by healing his servant (Luke 7:1-10).

Christ's love and compassion is full and boundless to everyone in need.

Christ's love and compassion is full and boundless to everyone in need. No one is excluded from His love! All you have to do is have an encounter with Jesus through faith in Him, and He will move on your behalf. Look at what He did for the widow of Nain.

"And he that was dead sat up, and began to speak. And he delivered him to his mother. And there came a fear on all: and they glorified God, saying, That a great prophet is risen up among us; and, That God hath visited his people." (Luke 7:15-16)

As noted earlier in the story of the Shunammite woman, we are to cast our cares on Him for He cares for us (1 Peter 5:7). In times of bereavement, many emotions transpire—disbelief, confusion, shock, sadness, anger—and experiencing these feelings is natural and healthy as you cope with your loss. However, with time and with God, you will get through it.

I remember when my oldest brother died from cancer. It was extremely difficult for me to accept because I had fervently prayed for his healing, not knowing that it was going to take place on the other side, in Heaven. I was angry at God because He did not heal him. I knew He could and believed He would. I had fasted and interceded and called on the elders of the church, but my brother died anyway. I was always so proud to tell others, "I have five brothers," but now I had only four, and the reality simply wouldn't register in my mind. My confusion was so great that I isolated myself for a time, speaking to no one. There was nothing anyone could say to me to bring me out of my funk.

Then God had me turn to the story of David and Bathsheba and the loss of their son (2 Samuel 12:15-23). David had fasted, sitting in sackcloth and ashes while the baby was sick, petitioning to God to heal his child—but when the infant died, David realized God had taken his son to Heaven. He got up, washed and anointed himself, changed his clothes, and went to the house of the Lord to worship before eating. I believe that David concluded that he would one day see his little boy again.

That story healed my heart and helped me to live on in peace. It showed me that even David did all He could to pray to the Lord, yet God's plan did not change. Everyone has a birthday and a death day. No one can escape either one. But as Christians, we know that when the tabernacle of our physical body is "dissolved, we have a building of God, an house not made with hands, eternal in the heavens." (2 Corinthians 5:1).

As I write this, I am facing the fact that my husband, Derek, after having ten strokes, is very sick, and I do not know what the outcome will be. However, I am still praying, fasting, and anointing him with oil for his complete healing. I see the hand of God moving on my husband's behalf because he is still here. He should've been dead, but God has spared his life. My husband's total dependence is in the Lord—and so is mine. Only God can mend a grief-stricken heart. I know because He has done it for me. Hold on to God when you are going through the death of someone dear to you. Draw close to God, and He will heal your heart and visit you.

DETERMINED PURSUIT: THE CANAANITE WOMAN

Another incredible woman Jesus visited—or rather, who visited Him—was the Canaanite woman (Matthew 15:21-28). She was a Gentile (in his Gospel, Mark identified her as being Syrophoenician) who was not only outside of the Jewish nation, but from a particular group of people who were especially despised and ostracized by them.

Still, that didn't prevent her from pursuing Christ, a Jewish rabbi, in desperate audacity.

"Lord, Son of David, have mercy on me! My daughter is demon-possessed and suffering terribly." (Matthew 15:21, NIV)

She may not have known it wasn't customary for a woman to ask anything of a rabbi, but she surely did know of the prejudice against her people. Yet she must've heard of Christ's ability to perform miracles, and that many of those He had healed were not Jews. Her plight was so dire she didn't care what anyone thought of her. Also, she may have called Jesus "Lord, Son of David" because she had heard of others who were healed use that terminology to refer to Him. Whatever the case, she came as a mother and pled for mercy, willing to do whatever it took to help her daughter.

Christ's response was most interesting—and surprising.

"Jesus did not answer a word. So his disciples came to him and urged him, 'Send her away, for she keeps crying out after us.'" (Matthew 15:22, NIV)

What? Christ did not reply? He had always shown such caring, thoughtful, and gentle compassion toward others in need, especially women. Yet here He seemed aloof, even harsh. Why?

Perhaps Jesus discerned that the woman needed deliverance just as much as her daughter did, not from a demon, but from her sins. Maybe He knew she was sincerely seeking Him on behalf of her daughter, but that she needed to go deeper and recognize her own need for Him. It could be that He wanted her to seek Him with everything she had so she could to receive everything He was: healer, deliverer, and Savior. That is, after all, what He wants from all of us. We are not to see God as some magic genie we can call upon to get what we want and then go about our ways. The Lord wants us to recognize Him as Lord over every part of our lives and to be women who seek Him not just for our needs, but to know Him as our Messiah through His Word, worship, and prayer.

We must care for all those who are in need of a Savior.

God knows if we are seeking Him superficially or sincerely. Just before the Canaanite woman's arrival, Jesus had spoken of those who "honor me with their lips, but their hearts are far from me." (Mark 7:6, NIV) He had gone on to say, "What comes out of a person is what defiles them. For it is from within, out of a person's heart, that evil thoughts come—sexual immorality, theft, murder, adultery, greed, malice, deceit, lewdness, envy, slander, arrogance and folly. All these evils come from inside and defile a person." (Mark 7:21-23, NIV)

I believe this was on Christ's mind as the Canaanite woman

called out to Him, but her cries had become so persistent that the disciples, knowing she was Syrophoenician, asked Him to dismiss her. I believe, too, that the disciples felt so arrogant toward her that they thought her cries included them when she was solely pleading for Jesus. In the same way, we can become so prideful in our own walk with Christ that we fail to show compassion because we do not want to be bothered or because we think that a person is not worthy of God's attention, much less His love. This cannot be so. We must care for all those who are in need of a Savior.

Next, Christ made a statement to His disciples and the others around Him, then responded to the woman herself as she finally caught up to Him.

> "He answered, 'I was sent only to the lost sheep of Israel.' The woman came and knelt before him. 'Lord, help me!' she said. He replied, 'It is not right to take the children's bread and toss it to the dogs.'" (Matthew 15:24-26, NIV)

I believe Jesus knew the woman needed to move some bitterness and pride in her life, perhaps caused by the way the Jews treated her, but why would Jesus treat her in such a manner? We are not told—but she had certainly heard Him tell everyone else that He had been sent "only to the lost sheep of Israel," a statement that undoubtedly made her feel like even more of an outsider.

But look at her persistence! She not only came up to Him, but she knelt before Him. She showed complete submission to Him in an exhibition of her desperation to recognize Him as Lord. She looked past all the prejudice, sexism, and even Christ's own discounting remarks. Why? I believe the Canaanite woman realized she was in the presence of the one true, living God!

Sometimes God will put us in a position where we will be brought to our knees before Him. Our prayers may not be answered right away, revealing our true character and trust in Him. Other times He will try to pull something out of us that may be hindering our ability to hear from Him. Will we turn and walk away, or will we continue to pursue? We will encounter many obstacles in this Christian life, but if we remain faithful and persistent, we will see the miracles of God.

Even in her humbled state, Christ challenged the Canaanite woman once more—and her response was nothing short of remarkable.

"He replied, 'It is not right to take the children's bread and toss it to the dogs.' 'Yes it is, Lord,' she said. 'Even the dogs eat the crumbs that fall from their master's table.'" (Matthew 15:26-27, NIV)

Wow! It is with her reply that she is brought to acceptance, for she acknowledged her own sinful condition. The moment you acknowledge that you are a sinner in need of a Savior is the moment when you have reached salvation. When you remove pride and self-centeredness, Jesus can move in your life. She broke through all the barriers—in the culture and in her heart—and in doing so she found a delivering Savior.

"Then Jesus said to her, 'Woman, you have great faith! Your request is granted.' And her daughter was healed at that moment." (Matthew 15:28, NIV)

Will you come to Jesus with pure faith in His ability to save you? Will you trust in His life sacrifice to give you life—and life more abundantly? Will you continue seeking after Him regardless of the obstacles? That's what the Canaanite woman did, and she was changed forever by her determined pursuit of God.

AGENDAS OVER COMPASSION: THE WOMAN CAUGHT IN ADULTERY

John 8:1-11 gives us a memorable account from Scripture found nowhere else in the Bible. In fact, it's likely one of the most recognizable and taught-upon stories in the Gospels. The two main characters are Jesus and an unnamed woman (some believe her to be Mary Magdalene, though there is no biblical support for this claim). The other players in the drama are the Jewish leaders, the scribes and Pharisees, who apparently caught this woman in the very act of adultery. How they did this we are not told. Nor is it revealed what they did with the man involved. What we do know is that adultery is a sinful transgression of the Jewish law punishable by death; in this case, by stoning (Leviticus 20:10, Deuteronomy 22:22). Under Roman law, the Jewish people were not allowed to carry out any punishment without approval from the governmental authorities, but they evaded the law when they chose.

The Jewish leaders had their own agenda for bringing the woman to Him. They were scheming to kill Jesus, and perhaps looked to further that desire by discrediting Christ using the Jewish or Roman law. Would Jesus appear to break Jewish law by not sanctioning her stoning? Would He seem to be affirming Roman law by preventing her death at their hands? Either way, the scribes and Pharisees made their move to trap Jesus by bringing her before Him while He was teaching to a large crowd in the temple.

Can you imagine what was going through this broken woman's mind as they dragged her into the temple? She surely knew the penalty for her sin and felt the harsh contempt the Jewish leaders felt toward her. Really, it was worse than contempt. She was merely a pawn in their strategy to take down Jesus. They cared nothing for her. We don't know for sure, but since they caught her in the act of adultery, it's possible she was naked or barely clothed as they brought her before Christ and the people. This would've added to her shame. She may have also been wondering about the man she was with when she was caught. Where was he? Did they just let him go free? Why wasn't he being punished? Finally, where was the respect for the temple of the Lord that the Jewish leaders should have had? How despicable, degrading, embarrassing, hateful, and hurtful they were—all in a desperate ploy to trip up Jesus. They willingly exploited her in their desire to get to Him.

I do not intend to excuse the woman's sin, but I have a huge problem with how the Jewish leaders handled this situation because it mirrors what still occurs in many churches today. When we as church leaders are more concerned about our own agendas than the well-being of another person, we have lost sight of Jesus' grace and mercy—and God is not pleased. In addition, how long will church leaders diminish or outright ignore the importance of women as individuals, as contributing members of the church community, or as leaders within the ministry of the church? Far too often, we still see women ostracized and even exploited—especially when it comes to the double standard that exists in churches when dealing with sexual sin. Time and again, we have witnessed adulterous men in churches, particularly in leadership, who are loved, forgiven, and restored while the women involved are branded as harlots (or worse) and are shunned by, or expelled from, the congregation. Men are constantly excused for their indiscretions. Even the wife who was innocently victimized by the adultery is usually left on her own to deal with the crisis, sitting silently as others stare or ridicule while her husband is being restored.

We see this all the time, but we never speak of it. Where do these women go? Who is ministering to them? No one cares. No one says a thing. They can't stay in their own church. They have to start all over and find a place where people don't know them. Such behavior in our churches is everything the Jewish leaders were in John 8.

Despicable. Degrading. Embarrassing. Hateful. Hurtful. When is this going to change? I don't know—but it must.

There's no doubt the woman in this story was a sinner, but look at how Jesus valued her life as a human being created in His image. At the very least, we should do the same. Women of substance are to be recognized, appreciated, and esteemed. We must lean on the Lord and on each other to make the right decisions for our lives and to live holy and righteous before God with discipline and commitment to His Word. Everything we do must be pleasing to the Lord more than pleasing to ourselves.

Everything we do must be pleasing to the Lord more than pleasing to ourselves.

So, what did Jesus do for this woman as the Jewish leaders bellowed for her death?

"Jesus stooped down, and with his finger wrote on the ground, as though he heard them not. So when they continued asking him, he lifted up himself, and said unto them, He that is without sin among you, let him first cast a stone at her. And again he stooped down, and wrote on the ground. And they which heard it, being convicted by their own conscience, went out one by one, beginning at the eldest, even unto the last: and Jesus was left alone, and the woman standing in the midst." (John 8:6-9)

Jesus did not acknowledge the men, though He was undoubtedly disgusted to see this kind of behavior going on in the temple. He did not ridicule the woman. No one knows what He wrote on the ground, but I believe it was the names of the individuals there who had committed the same sin of adultery, as well as who they were with when they did. That is the only way I can see how

119

these men, full of hatred and malice, would abort their evil plot by throwing down their stones and leaving as quickly as they had arrived.

Then, when only the woman and Jesus remained, they had a brief dialogue. It was beautiful and overflowing with compassion.

"When Jesus had lifted up himself, and saw none but the woman, he said unto her, Woman, where are those thine accusers? hath no man condemned thee? She said, No man, Lord. And Jesus said unto her, Neither do I condemn thee: go, and sin no more." (John 8:10-11)

Jesus loved her.
Jesus forgave her.
Jesus restored *her*.

Dear God, may we do the same for broken women in our midst. May abuses against women in the church and anywhere else cease. May women never be devalued among your people. This is so far off from your plan for your children. It is a reflection of what happens in the world. Yet Jesus came to liberate us from the world, so we would behave as individuals worthy of His love and grace. May the Christian church model your behavior, Lord, toward the woman caught in adultery. Let us not allow our own iniquities to get in the way of seeing you, God, and your plan for our lives. Amen.

PART THREE

How Important We Are to God's Purposes

Chapter 8

"Neither shall they say, Lo here! or, lo there! for,
behold, the kingdom of God is within you."
(Luke 17:21)

As women of substance, we've learned who we are in God and how important we are to Him. Now, we'll discover how important we are to God's Kingdom purposes for our lives. Psalm 57:2 exhorts, "Cry unto God most high; unto God that performeth all things for me." The Lord works all things according to His purposes in His Kingdom, which is defined as the spiritual realm over which God reigns as king, and is manifested as the accomplishment of God's will on Earth. It is in this Kingdom that we operate as daughters of the King; therefore, it is *through us* that His purposes are fulfilled—for ourselves and in the lives of those we touch.

We are important to the Lord's Kingdom purposes in all stages of our lives, but I'm going to focus specifically on the different Kingdom purposes fulfilled by both married and single women. Each of them are equally valuable and vital.

MARRIED WOMEN:
AN ESSENTIAL PRESENCE FOR HER FAMILY

Proverbs 18:22 declares, "Whoso findeth a wife findeth a good thing, and obtaineth favour of the Lord." A wife brings favor to her husband. She is a blessing to him because she is *already* equipped by the Lord to be a wife and is guided by the Holy Spirit. Titus 2:3-4 teaches us that it is through the example of truthful, holy,

123

and sober elder women, combined with God's divine intervention, that a woman of substance is shaped into a wife before she ever says, "I do." The wisdom, insight, common sense, and understanding of her family and her gifts in ministry all derive from the input of older women and discernment from God.

A wife's foremost ministry is to her husband and children. According to God's Kingdom purposes, she is to help, love, and support her husband in ministry, home life, work, and everyday life expectancies. A wife's care for her husband and family is essential to the progression of the Kingdom of God on Earth. Titus 2:5 says a wife is to be "discreet, chaste, keepers at home, good, obedient to their own husbands, that the word of God be not blasphemed." A wife is purposed by God to be self-controlled, morally good, and possessing a good character that reflects the character of God. She is also to be pure, have integrity, and be busy at home to ensure it is intact and lacking nothing. This is achieved through various roles, from giving spiritual counsel and pouring life and love into her children, to keeping a clean home, and cooking for and feeding her husband and family. A Kingdom-purpose wife is kind to everyone, especially her family, and she is subject to her husband, meaning that no other man should have influence over her. Anything else would discredit the words of God.

> *A wife's care for her husband and family is essential to the progression of the Kingdom of God on Earth.*

Finally, since there is only one King on Heaven's throne, a wife should inspire her husband and speak to the king in him. The husband's role in his family is just as important as the wife's. Just as we are to share in the duties of the ministry of God, we also must share the responsibility of meeting the spiritual health and well-being of the family.

In today's society where so many women have professional careers, caring for our family and supporting our husband is frowned upon. But if we understand that this is God's Kingdom purpose for our lives, then we will be pleasing to Him. That is more important than any career choice, but don't misunderstand. I am not saying that women cannot have a professional career. Remember the Proverbs 31 woman profiled earlier? She was an entrepreneur, successful in her business and in her community, her husband was well known (had favor), and her children admired her. A woman who fears the Lord can have a husband, children, and a career—and still be fully operating in His Kingdom purposes.

You may be a superintendent of a school district, or a lawyer, doctor, or CEO of a large company. Whatever your gifting, God will give you, as a wife, the wisdom to manage it all and keep things in order while keeping your family as your first priority. That will give you the opportunity to exhibit the characteristics of God and to do good for others.

Just think: if every married woman lived her life according to the Bible, the world would have less crime, abuse, and immorality because her influence as a wife and mother would be imprinted on the psyche of her family. That is how powerful a wife can be.

SINGLE WOMEN:
GREAT PURPOSE IN THE KINGDOM OF GOD

Women who are single and love the Lord are in the best position to give glory to God because their time and heart are not as divided as they are in women who have a husband or children. The Bible declares that "a woman who is no longer married or has never been married can be devoted to the Lord and holy in body and in spirit" while "a married woman has to think about her earthly responsibilities and how to please her husband." (1 Corinthians

7:34, NLT) Therefore, a single woman does not have to split her time between family and God. She can be totally committed to ministry and establish herself in her career, education, hobbies, and socialization. That enables her to be one of the greatest assets to the Kingdom of God because her full liberty is in the Lord. A single woman can build the Kingdom through teaching, ministering, witnessing, sharing her gifts, and being an example. The four daughters of Philip (Acts 21:9) were single women who were powerful in their spiritual gifts and who devoted their lives to ministry. They were virgins with the gift of prophecy. We don't know their names or the details of their lives, but we can infer that they were effective in ministry through their mention in the Scriptures.

As a young person, when I first accepted the Lord as my Savior, I was determined to tell everyone about my encounter with the Lord. I witnessed about the goodness of God to my friends, family, neighbors, co-workers, and even people in my church. To His glory, many people accepted the Lord because of my testimony. I was a youth leader, choir member, and district youth president in our association. I went to as many worship services and Bible studies as I could. I saturated myself in ministry. If I was not in school or at work, I was somewhere enjoying doing ministry.

During that time, I chose to date a gentleman who was not saved, and he became jealous of the church and its prominence in my life. I constantly invited him to church and functions being held there, but he would not attend. Early in our relationship, I explained to him that I was going to abstain from sex because I was committed to be holy in both body and spirit. He didn't understand or agree, and it was a problem for him. It wasn't until he realized that I was serious about my decision that he conceded and let it go. He was also in a baseball league, and his team played on Tuesday nights. He wanted me to attend his games, but because that was youth night, I could never make it to one. One evening, he called me with an ultimatum. "You need to choose between the youth or me. All of the players have their wives and girlfriends in the stands but me, and I want you to be there to support me."

As he spoke, I understood for the first time the scripture from 2 Corinthians 6:14-15.

"Do not be bound together with unbelievers; for what partnership have righteousness and lawlessness, or what fellowship has light with darkness? Or what harmony has Christ with Belial, or what has a believer in common with an unbeliever?" (NASB)

It was not biblical to be dating someone who did not believe or serve God as I did. Because I was not sexually active with him, and therefore, not bound to him with a "soul tie" (defined as a spiritual connection between two people who have been physically intimate with each other or who have had an intense emotional or spiritual association or relationship), it was easy to maintain God first in my life, even when he complained about it. Besides, the relationship was going nowhere, and I knew it was time to make a decision. That night, I called back to let him know we needed to meet, and I broke off the relationship.

Dating relationships are the number one problem facing single Christian women. We tend to prioritize a man over ministry as though he is our husband, but until you say "I do" before a minister and a room of witnesses, you are not obligated to *him*. You are *only* obligated to God. You must know your convictions and set your standards according to the Word of God—and then stand by them, no matter what! My mistake was in choosing to date the guy in the first place, but my convictions kept me from getting into trouble with him, myself, and with God.

Find your gifts in ministry, put your mind, body, and soul into them, and get busy for the Lord! Attend Bible studies, join Christian singles groups, and learn how a single woman should live in the eyes of the Lord. Keep yourself chaste so that you can make sound and godly decisions. As a single woman, you can give more to ministry and saving others than any other person in the body of Christ. You are so valuable—and the Kingdom needs you.

SINGLE WOMEN WITH CHILDREN: A SPECIAL CASE

While other single women do not carry the burden of traditional family responsibilities, a single woman with children is a whole other matter. Many fit this category today, and even though the husband/father is gone, single mothers have a responsibility to their children which will divide the time they can dedicate to ministry. Their greatest responsibility is to take care of their children, raise them in the admonition of the Lord, and to trust God to be Father, provider, and protector over the household.

On several occasions, I have seen single women prioritize ministry over their children's well-being. That is a mistake. It can cause resentment from their children and neglect to their emotional and spiritual development. While it is good to be involved in church ministry, their children must also have a life outside of the church, in the home, and at their schools. So, just like the married woman, a single mother's first responsibility is to impart love, morals, kindness, and all the attributes of God to her children and family.

> *A single mother's first responsibility is to impart love, morals, kindness, and all the attributes of God to her children and family.*

In 2 Timothy 1:5, Paul wrote of the tremendous impact Timothy's grandmother Lois and mother Eunice had on Timothy's life. Both were devout Jewish women who converted to Christianity once the Gospel was preached to them. Paul commended them on how well they taught the Word of God to Timothy, who became a powerful leader in the early Church. Paul only mentioned Timothy's father as being a Gentile and gave all of the credit for Timothy's upbringing to these two women. This suggests that Timothy's father may have been deceased or was out of the picture for some other reason. Whether Eunice was a widow or abandoned by her husband in some other way, she was a single mother and her devotion was to her son and her family.

A MERCHANT WITH DIVINE PURPOSE: LYDIA

Lydia was a worshipper of the Lord and a successful businesswoman. There is no mention of her being married, and based on how she earned her living, she was either unmarried or a widow. She had traveled from her hometown of Thyatira to the Roman colony of Philippi because, as a successful merchant, she knew her product and her market. Renowned as "a seller of purple," (Acts 16:14) her quality cloths and textiles were in high demand—especially those dyed purple that were worn by dignitaries and royal families.

But what profited Lydia most in Philippi that day was ultimately far more valuable than the sale of her fabrics. Already a worshiper of God, Lydia was introduced to Paul, who in turn introduced her to Jesus Christ. She was converted at the riverside where she overheard Paul, Silas, and some other disciples explaining the Gospel. God opened her heart to receive what was being said (Acts 16:14), and she and her household, possibly containing children and servants, were immediately baptized. Look at the great influence she had on her family! Her love for God and the testimony of her conversion inspired them to believe.

Recognized as the very first Christian convert in Europe, she immediately wanted to serve God and boldly offered her home to Paul, Silas, and Timothy. Lydia ministered to the men of God, and she was persistent and determined to be of help to those who labored for Christ. She became known for her financial, spiritual, and physical contributions to the church, using her wealth, influence, and home to give back to the God who so faithfully gave to her. In fact, that home became a regular meeting place for believers and likely, scholars speculate, the very birthplace of the Philippian church.

Lydia was committed to God and did not allow her work or other obligations to get in the way of her worship. God's purpose for Lydia's life was to help support the new church, keep it progressing, and see it multiply throughout the world as Lydia fulfilled His purpose for her life.

What is your purpose in the Kingdom of God? Everyone has one. Lydia was moved by God to walk in her purpose. It is what you give, out of the sincere love of your heart, that directs you to your purpose. Continue to worship God. There is so much He will reveal to you.

FROM ADVERSITY TO PURPOSE: NAOMI

Naomi and her daughter-in-law, Ruth, had completely different backgrounds, yet they were both strong, determined women who were totally committed to one another. The book of Ruth starts out with our introduction to Naomi, her husband, Elimelech, and her two sons living in Bethlehem during a famine. A devoted wife, Naomi followed her husband to the foreign country of Moab to escape the famine and save their family. At the time, Elimelech surely thought it was a good idea, but they left Bethlehem (the "house of bread" in Hebrew) to go to Moab. Pastor, Bible teacher, theologian, and radio minister J. Vernon McGee of Thru the Bible noted in one of his commentaries that Psalm 108:9 referred to Moab as a "washpot," adding that the Moabites were an outcast people with a sordid and sorry beginning (Genesis 19:30-37). They were also an enemy to the Israelites and constantly worshipped idols.

Although Naomi believed in her husband and her God, when tragedy hit her home and family, she lost all hope. Shortly after arriving in Moab, her husband died. Although her sons took care of her and eventually married two Moabite women, Ruth and Orpah, both sons died a decade later. I can see how Naomi became hopeless. She lost everything: the husband she loved and trusted and the two sons she birthed and once held at her bosom. All three were gone, never to return, and she was in a foreign land with no family, no money, and no security. Yes, Naomi still had her daughters-in-law, but in that culture, women were left desolate without males in their families. Naomi's future looked very bleak.

Even worse, though, was how Naomi looked upon herself and her Lord. She felt God had been harsh with her and that she was being punished. But she still had powerful, motherly love for Ruth and Orpah and chose to look ahead to their futures despite believing that there was no future left for her. What incredible love she showed for her daughters-in-law, realizing that her desires for them would leave her all alone and helpless. Naomi knew that if they followed her back home to Bethlehem, they would not have husbands in their future because no Israelite man would ever marry a Moabite woman.

So, in the middle of her suffering, bitterness, and tragedy, Naomi took the time to look after Ruth and Orpah, telling them to go back to their homes in Moab where they could be with their own family and friends. Naomi loved them, and they loved her. Incredibly, Ruth refused to leave Naomi's side, and she stayed and cared for her mother-in-law throughout Naomi's journey back to her homeland of Bethlehem where she could find some comfort in familiar surroundings. When the duo arrived in Bethlehem, the scars of Naomi's tragedy were shown in her countenance. The women who were once her friends were amazed to see Naomi in such bad shape. They could not believe it was her. Naomi was so distraught that she changed her name.

"Call me not Naomi, call me Mara: for the Almighty hath dealt very bitterly with me." (Ruth 1:20)

Her great loss had taken her to a place of depression, uncertainty, and grief. Still, Naomi must have called to mind the commandment God had given the Israelites about their responsibility to care for widows, orphans, and strangers (Deuteronomy 24:19-22). Though she felt abandoned by the Lord, Naomi understood that God saw her and Ruth as being among the most vulnerable of people, so He made provision for them. In truth, the Lord had not abandoned Naomi at all. He was patient and provided for her all along the way. God understood her feelings of despair and brought comfort to her through Ruth. God will always provide for His daughters. Just look! The provision is there.

There may come a time when you are hit with the most devastating trauma of your life—yet must depend on the Lord to get you through. Naomi's story was very difficult for me to write because I can relate to her pain. In Chapter 7, I shared how my husband, Derek, was very sick and that we were trusting God for his healing. But on January 31, 2020, at the age of 56, God called him home. I was devastated because I expected the Lord to heal him on this side of Heaven, not on the other side. When you lose a spouse, that is a pain only God can heal. No one can comfort you or mend the brokenness you are experiencing. In my soul, I had to discover how to live this life without Derek. We did everything together. He was my soulmate, the one God chose for me. He loved me with an unconditional love, the love Christ had for His Church. Derek was the one who encouraged me to write this book, and to do it for His Kingdom purposes, when I felt I was not worthy or qualified to do so.

I asked the Lord, "How can I go on without him by my side? What will I become?" I gave my life to the Lord at the age of 21, and by the time I was 22, I had met Derek. We were married two years later, so most of my Christian life has been shared with my hus-

Depend on the Lord to get you through.

band. But as my grief counselor, Manuel Costa, told me, "Derek still loves you because love is a spirit that never dies. Your love for him and his love for you still exists. Find comfort in this." As I was reading the Word of God one day following Derek's death, the Holy Spirit came to me in a still, small voice as I was studying about prayer. I wasn't seeking the Lord specifically for Derek in any way. The Spirit said, "For one whole year, it was me and you. We spent intimate time together, and you became my daughter. Then you asked me for a husband, and I gave you Derek as a gift from me. You both spent 31 years serving me and walking in holy matrimony, building the Kingdom of God. He has completed his assignment. Now it is just you and me once again—and I will take care of you just like I have done all of your life. You have purpose."

God knew what was in my heart, even though I had not audibly asked Him for anything. He provided exactly what I needed, and it gave me comfort and assurance that I would indeed be able to go on without my husband. It can be easy to find yourself in the same hopeless state Naomi was, but you don't have to stay there. There are five stages of grief, according to psychiatrist Elisabeth Kübler-Ross, author of *On Death and Dying*: denial, anger, bargaining, depression, and acceptance. You may or may not experience all of these stages, and for you, they may come in a different order. But when and if you are going through these stages, be assured they are a normal part of the healing process.

I encourage you to stay in contact with someone you can easily talk to and who will listen and allow you to grieve. It is also important to have emotional and physical support from family and friends. They will be your inner group. When you feel like being alone, that's fine, but be careful not to isolate yourself too long. Allow others to visit and comfort you, and even give yourself permission to smile. Get out and take walks or a drive. Identify small or big projects to do to help you fill idle time, and if you are employed, go back to work when you are ready.

Seek and receive some type of counseling from your pastor or a professional grief counselor. This is so important for your spiritual and mental well-being because you will ask many questions as you grieve. Remember, too, that God understands how you feel and that it is okay to ask questions of Him. Read the Word of God and talk to Him about everything you are feeling. He will hear your every cry—and remember, crying is an essential way to grieve and heal. Scriptures to help you through times of grief include Psalm 23, Psalm 34:18, Psalm 73:26, Psalm 119:28, Psalm 147:3, Isaiah 26:3-4, Isaiah 40:31, Isaiah 41:10, John 14:17, 2 Corinthians 1:34, 2 Corinthians 5:1 and 8, and 1 Thessalonians 4:13-14 and 31.

I still miss Derek terribly, but I know he is very much alive and healed in Heaven, loving me with a love that will never die. One day, we will be united once again. I thank God that I did not get to the place Naomi did. Despair and hopelessness are a terrible place to be, and they only lead you further away from seeing God's love for you. Today, the Lord is sustaining me, and I can feel His love covering me. He is my strength, my peace, my comfort, and my friend. I know He understands what I am experiencing because of Hebrews 4:15-16, which declares of Jesus,

"We don't have a priest who is out of touch with our reality. He's been through weakness and testing, experienced it all—all but the sin. So let's walk right up to him and get what he is so ready to give. Take the mercy, accept the help." (MSG)

Since Derek's death, I have rested my head on God's bosom, and He is caring for me, strengthening me, and comforting me to health. The Lord is the one who gave me the strength to complete this book, reminding me that I am made of a substance that can withstand anything. As we fuse that strength with the Holy Spirit, we will be made whole.

If you have encountered a loss in your family, trust and lean on the Lord your God and allow Him to minister to you. Take time to heal. Do not rush it. Stay focused on Him—and get up and live! There is much more for you to do in this world and for His Kingdom. Have faith that God will bring you through, and day by day you will feel yourself getting stronger. Seek the Lord each and every day, listen for His instruction, and obey. He knows what you need.

In the end, going back home was the best thing Naomi ever did. She did not give up and die in Moab. She muscled up the strength to travel back home where God took over and carried out His amazing providence in her and through her. Naomi had incredible purpose. She was the agent who brought Ruth and Boaz, a kinsman of her husband's, together. Through their union, Obed, the grandfather of King David, was born. Not only did Ruth continue to treat Naomi as a beloved mother, but God performed a miracle for Naomi that allowed her to nurse little Obed. She took care of him as her son, so that even the women in her country declared that God had blessed her with another son—and not just any, but one through whose lineage the promised Messiah, Jesus Christ, would come (Ruth 4:14-22).

So hold on, my sisters in Christ! God has a perfect outcome in every situation, just as Jeremiah 29:11-13 promises.

"'For I know the plans I have for you,' declares the Lord, 'plans to prosper you and not to harm you, plans to give you hope and a future. Then you will call on me and come and pray to me, and I will listen to you. You will seek me and find me when you seek me with all your heart.'" (NIV)

PURE, SELFLESS LOVE: RUTH

Ruth was a woman of strength, honor, commitment, compassion, loyalty, and hope. She was beautiful both inside and out, and another example of a true woman of substance who lived out her purpose despite great personal tragedy. Most of all, Ruth fell in love with the true and living God of the universe, and she showed that love to an elder woman of God who had lost all hope.

Ruth's story begins as she meets and marries a foreigner living in her country, Moab. Unfortunately, she became a widow at an early age. But before the death of her husband, Mahlon, Ruth must have decided to deny all of Moab's idol worship and their false gods to follow the God of her husband and his family. We see this in her declaration to her mother-in-law, Naomi, as they journeyed back to Judah. In the middle of their journey, Naomi urgently told both Ruth and her other daughter-in-law, Orpah, to go back to their country to remarry and have families of their own. She convincingly painted a bleak and desperate picture of their future they chosen to remain with her. Though Orpah loved Naomi, she decided to go back to Moab—but Ruth's love both for Naomi and for God was more profound and tied to something bigger than herself. She revealed it in her declaration to Naomi.

"But Ruth said, 'Do not urge me to leave you or to return from following you. For where you go I will go, and where you lodge I will lodge. Your people shall be my people, and your God my God. Where you die I will die, and there will I be buried. May the Lord do so to me and more also if anything but death parts me from you.'" (Ruth 1:16-17, ESV)

Incredible, isn't it? Ruth had made up her mind long before they came to this fork in the road. She had decided that the God of Israel was going to be her God, the one she would serve and love with her whole being. Before Naomi encountered her bitter state, she must have had a great influence on Ruth to cause her to place God so deeply in her heart. Ruth's love for her mother-in-law was not the norm for most daughter-in-law / mother-in-law relationships then or today, but Naomi made it easy for both Orpah and Ruth to love her because of the love she poured out on them. Yet with Ruth, we see a pure, selfless love, and she was determined that nothing was going to separate her from Naomi or her God. Ruth denounced everything of her country and devoted her heart to the Lord. She did not look back, but instead, gazed forward to living and loving God and her mother-in-law in the land of the Hebrews.

I want to point out that the love Ruth was exhibiting is the kind of love Jesus asks us to have—to love the Lord with all of our heart, soul, and mind, and to love our neighbors as ourselves (Matthew 22:37-40), selflessly and sacrificially. Ruth gave up her life, family, and country. Can you see it? This is what God is asking from us as women of substance. Our minds must be settled so that, no matter what happens, we will always keep our love, commitment, and honor for God with true, devoted hearts. Ruth's story shows us how to love God and our neighbors, because anyone we come in contact with is our neighbor.

Paul talks about God's love for us in Romans 8:37-39.

"None of this fazes us because Jesus loves us. I'm absolutely convinced that nothing—nothing living or dead, angelic or demonic, today or tomorrow, high or low, thinkable or unthinkable—absolutely *nothing* can get between us and God's love because of the way that Jesus our Master has embraced us." (MSG)

Ruth was a living testimony of this scripture, and it conveys what she was communicating to Naomi through her actions about her commitment to her, and now, their God. Like Ruth, we feel the love of God. It fuses us to Him, and nothing comes between us and God's love toward us. It's that kind of love that makes us more than conquerors though Christ (Romans 8:37), and it is that kind of love that will carry us through the roughest situations and still come out victorious. It is all because of what Jesus did for us, and how His love for us kept Him focused on the plan of salvation revealed in Romans 5:8. "But God demonstrates his own love for us in this: While we were still sinners, Christ died for us." (NIV)

Ruth's love for Naomi also gave her an intimate understanding of Naomi's pain which caused her to empathize with Naomi and even carry her toward her purpose. Ruth did not allow Naomi's bitterness to get in the way of pressing forward with her. She still saw Naomi as a woman of love, patience, and acceptance, even in her bitterness. Only God can implant such love in our hearts that we allow the Holy Spirit to help us feel the pain of others, have empathy for them, and not give up on them. All of us should desire to love God and others as Ruth did and as 1 Peter 4:8-9 declares. "Above all things have fervent charity [love] among yourselves: for charity shall cover the multitude of sins. Use hospitality one to another without grudging."

> *All of us should desire to love God and others.*

When Ruth and Naomi arrived in Bethlehem, they had no food, no shelter, and no male to care for them. They were poor, destitute, and at the mercy of those who would give alms to them. Their future looked bleak—but remember that God made provision for them through His commandment to the Israelites in Deuteronomy 24:19-22 to care for widows, orphans, and strangers. Verse 19 stated, "When you harvest your grain and forget a sheaf back in the field, don't go back and get it; leave it for the foreigner, the orphan, and the widow so that God, your God, will bless you in all your work." (MSG)

God makes provision for the less fortunate. If that is you today, don't give up! The Lord will make a way for you.

He certainly did for Ruth. She was a foreigner and a widow, yet she remained determined to take care of herself and her mother-in-law. So, Ruth decided to go out to glean, or gather, what was left in the fields (Ruth 2:2). This part of Ruth's story reminds me of the time my husband and I rented a house in San Jose. It was a month-to-month lease, and after we had lived there for two years, the landlord decided that she was going to sell the house to a relative. We were given just 30 days to move out. Devastated, we began looking for another house to rent in San Jose and around the Bay Area, but we couldn't find anything. We resorted to settling for an apartment so we could move out of the house in time, but even then, no one would rent to us. I was worried, and my husband was quiet. I knew that meant he was praying.

With the 30 days just about up, I said to Derek, "Maybe God wants us to buy a house."

He looked at me as though I had lost my mind. We barely had the money to rent another home or apartment, much less buy a house. But all I knew was that those doors were closed, and buying was the only thing we had not yet investigated.

Those 30 days turned to 45, and the landlord was adamant

that we had to leave. One Sunday morning while we were getting dressed for church, a sheriff's deputy came knocking at the door. We were so afraid we didn't answer, but when the deputy departed, he'd left behind a letter of eviction. It said we had 30 days to move, or they were going to do the moving for us.

I began to cry, asking God why this was happening. It seemed so unfair and so out of our control. I knew we could move in with my parents if we had to, but my husband wasn't happy with the idea. Derek went on to church, and I told him I would meet him there. After he left, I fell to my knees and started earnestly praying to God for help. I did not know where to go or what to do next.

I got up, went to my car, and started driving to church—but I just happened to travel a different route than I usually took. I had never gone that way before, and I don't know why I did then. As I was going down a long street in my neighborhood, I spied a house at the end of the corner with a little red, black, and white sign in the front window. It read HOUSE FOR SALE. I immediately stopped the car, got out, and walked up to the door. An older Caucasian woman answered, and I asked about the house. She asked me in, introduced herself as Susan, and proceeded to give me a tour. I felt that I had to be fully forthcoming with Susan, so I told her all about the eviction and the circumstances around it. I also shared how my husband and I did not have the money to buy a home, but we were waiting for God to provide for us.

Instantly, she said, "This is your house, and God is going to make a way for you." Then Susan added, "I am a Christian, too, and my prayer is that my husband will be saved. Come back this afternoon with your husband, and let's talk. Also, will you pray with me for my husband to be saved?"

Without hesitation, I told her I would—and we did, right there in the living room.

When I got to church, I couldn't wait to tell Derek what had happened.

"Elaine," he said, "you know we don't have the money to buy a house."

"I know," I said, "but God does!"

We went back after church to meet both Susan and her husband, Joe. As Derek again told them our story, Joe showed all of us around the house. When we went outside into the backyard, Joe and Derek walked up to the beautiful, brick barbeque pit Joe had built that extended across the entire patio. Derek loved it, and the two men bonded around that barbeque area.

Joe then spoke up. "We will give you the down payment for the house, and you can move in immediately. You can rent until the escrow goes through."

It was a miracle! Derek and I began to cry in the car as we drove home. We were so amazed at God's provision and how He had pushed us into our blessing. We didn't have a loan then, but we applied for one and it was quickly approved. We purchased our first home—and I still live in it today. We paid back the money we owed to Susan and Joe and became good friends with them. We lost touch many years later after they moved out of state. Susan never confirmed if her husband accepted the Lord, but I feel in my heart that he did. We were all blessed by God's providence. Nothing just happens!

As Ruth went out to glean the leftover grain remaining in the fields in Ruth 2, her upright character was evidenced as she asked the foreman for permission to gather, even though the right to do so was fully hers under God's law. She worked hard and long for the food needed for her and Naomi. But look at the providence of God! She just happened to end up in the field of Boaz, a very rich and God-fearing man—and a relative of Naomi's deceased husband. When Boaz saw Ruth in the field, he immediately inquired about her. At that moment, the two did not know they were distant relatives—and the answer to prayer.

Boaz was impressed by Ruth's devotion and commitment both to Naomi and to God. He had heard of their misfortune, so he made sure that she was provided for. In fact, Boaz told his workers to leave more harvest behind for Ruth to gather. He also instructed her to not go into any other field so she would be safe. This prevented her from possibly being raped by men who believed she had no protection. Boaz also took the time to get to know Ruth by having lunch with her. When Ruth arrived home with an abundance of barley and food from her lunch with Boaz, Naomi questioned who was being so nice to her. Ruth told her the man's name—and Naomi found hope once more.

> "Naomi said to her daughter-in-law, 'Why, God bless that man! God hasn't quite walked out on us after all! He still loves us, in bad times as well as good!' Naomi went on, 'That man, Ruth, is one of our circle of covenant redeemers, a close relative of ours!'" (Ruth 2:20, MSG)

Naomi saw the hand of God in everything that Ruth had told her. She also knew that Boaz, being a distant relative, could marry Ruth and provide for her. He was clearly interested in Ruth's well-being. Boaz sought Ruth out, provided for her, then communed with her and provided protection.

This is how God treats us. He first loved us (1 John 4:19), and He provides everything we need physically, mentally, emotionally, and spiritually. God communes with us and develops an intimate relationship with us that envelops us in His spiritual protection, making us one of His own. God's love keeps on providing for us, too. It is never ending.

Ruth had everything she needed to survive when she met Boaz—and so do we when we meet Jesus.

Next, Naomi instructed Ruth on how to let Boaz know she was interested in him. In her wisdom, Naomi told Ruth step-by-step how to obtain a husband, and Ruth trusted her and did exactly what she said (Ruth 3:1-15). It is so vital to have an elder woman in your life, especially a woman who has the wisdom of God. If you need it, she can help you choose the right man for your life. As you take heed to her instructions, you will be blessed.

God's love keeps on providing for us, too. It is never ending.

Naomi helped Ruth gain her husband, identified in the Bible as her kinsman redeemer. Jesus is your kinsmen redeemer. He bought you with a price, His life, while you were in a state of separation from God. He brought you back together with the Father and saved you from eternal damnation though His shed blood. This is what Boaz did for Ruth. He purchased the land from Elimelech's inheritance, which included Ruth (Ruth 4:9-10), and became her husband, saving her from complete destitution.

But this was no mere transaction. Though Scripture does not explicitly say, I believe Ruth loved Boaz, and he loved her. Ruth married Boaz, and their love for one another was evidenced by the fact that they had a child together: Obed, who would become the grandfather of King David. Even more, Ruth loved Naomi so much that she was given a vital role in raising the child (Ruth 4:14-17).

Ruth was a phenomenal woman who knew how to love and care for others. God restored her and gave her a husband and a child. God gave Ruth the best—and she gave Him her best: her whole heart, soul, and mind.

Chapter 9

"Create in me a clean heart, O God;
and renew a right spirit within me."
(Psalm 51:10)

As women of substance, we deal with various issues in our lives. They may be medical, mental, emotional, or relational. Some of these issues are lengthy and painful, and it's possible they've even made us outcasts in some way. They can be overwhelming— but that doesn't mean they have to overcome us. We can still find hope and strength as we acknowledge our issues, turn to Jesus, trust in Him, and allow Him to use them to take us to the next level of relationship and maturity in Him.

In Mark 5, we find Jesus busily ministering. It begins with Christ casting a legion of demons out of a man and into a herd of swine. After that, a synagogue ruler named Jairus came to Jesus, pleading with him to help his daughter, who was at the point of death. Christ decided to accompany Jairus to his home, and they were joined by a huge throng of people. They were surrounding Jesus, and I can picture them pushing and shoving to receive something from Him. There were far too many people for them to maintain a respectable distance, but Jesus was determined to make it to the sick daughter. Even the large crowds and the slow movement delaying His arrival were not going to deter Christ from His mission.

However, on His way to perform one miracle, another miracle

took place—and we are introduced to our next incredible woman of substance. Scripture identified her as "a certain woman, which had an issue of blood twelve years, And had suffered many things of many physicians, and had spent all that she had, and was nothing bettered, but rather grew worse." (Mark 5:25-26) The Bible doesn't mention her by name, but in her anonymity, this woman represents all of us so well.

She was at the end of her rope. All her money was gone, she was a social outcast separated from her family and friends, and she was deathly ill, in great pain, and most likely unable to even stand upright to walk up to Jesus. She had been tormented physically, mentally and socially by her "issue" of blood, a menstrual cycle condition so severe that it prevented her from being around others. Therefore, she was considered unclean under Hebrew law, as laid out in Leviticus 15:25. "When a woman has a discharge of blood for many days at a time other than her monthly period or has a discharge that continues beyond her period, she will be unclean as long as she has the discharge, just as in the days of her period." (NIV)

Despite that, this woman never gave up hope, and now she was willing to break through any and all barriers to get to Jesus. She did not care about what others thought of her or about the large crowd that prevented her from speaking with Christ. With nothing left but her faith, she said to herself, "If I may touch but his clothes, I shall be whole." (Mark 5:28)

Perhaps this remarkable woman decided to only touch His clothes out of respect for Christ, knowing that she had a blood issue that made her unclean. We don't know. What we can assume, however, is that she had already heard about Jesus and all the miracles He had performed. So have you—but have you acknowledged your issue and pressed in to Jesus? Have you done all you can and used all your strength to get close to Him? That's faith in action, and action is required. You need to *do* something about your issue to receive healing and wholeness. As James 2:26 tells us, "For as the body apart from the spirit is dead, so also faith apart from works is dead." (ESV) Your faith will lead you to the healing of your issue.

The woman with the issue of blood believed—and *acted* on that belief—that if she could just *touch* the hem of His garment, she would be made whole.

Not could. Would.

All too often, we want to ask Jesus to heal our issues, but we lack the faith to follow through to get to Him. Yet there is no issue too dark or too ugly that Christ cannot heal it. There is no one too far gone that Jesus cannot save. If you simply put your faith in action, this story tells you that you will be made whole. Maybe you need to find a healthy church home with like-minded people, befriend a wise elder woman to walk with you, go to a Bible study, have a devotion time with the Lord, or get active in ministry, even if that ministry is to clean the church's bathrooms. Your actions do not save you. Faith alone does. But your faith gives you the *desire* to give back to the Kingdom while moving closer to Jesus as you are being made whole.

That's what happened to the woman.

"When she had heard of Jesus, came in the press behind, and touched his garment. For she said, If I may touch but his clothes, I shall be whole. And straightway the fountain of her blood was dried up; and she felt in her body that she was healed of that plague." (Mark 5:27-29)

She had the substance to get to Jesus, but it was her faith that made her whole—and instantly, she was healed! Wow!

It makes me think back to the time when my husband came to Christ. Not long after we first met, I invited Derek, through his mother who was a member of our church, to be my guest and attend a youth church revival led by a special speaker, Pastor John W. Waiters. Derek was addicted to crack cocaine, and I knew God could heal him. Derek told me after the service that the only reason he agreed to come was to use his mother's car to visit the dope dealer that night after the service. Derek was even high when he arrived for the revival.

But he wasn't high by the time it was done. God, by His divine virtue, healed and delivered Derek at that service. When the pastor gave the altar call, he asked the congregation, "Aren't you tired of the life you have been living?" Derek said he felt like the pastor was talking directly to him, and something began to stir in his heart. Next thing he knew, he was standing up, and the pastor asked Derek to come forward. My husband later told me, "By that time, I knew that if I could just get to the front of the church and take the pastor by the hand, my life would never be the same."

He was right! Derek was immediately changed! He gave his whole heart to God—and from that night until the day he went home to glory, Derek did not smoke crack or touch any other drug again. He never had to attend a rehabilitation center or enter a 12-step program. He just began pouring himself into ministry and studying the Word of God, learning all about the Lord and what He expected of him. Even more amazing than the miracle of being healed from drug addiction, Derek's heart, mind, and soul were healed as well!

As Jesus heals you of your issue, He'll also fully restore your heart, mind, and soul.

As Jesus heals you of your issue, He'll also fully restore your heart, mind, and soul—and that change will be ongoing as you grow in Christ and the peace of God starts to guard your whole being. Jesus promised, "Peace I leave with you, my peace I give unto you: not as the world giveth, give I unto you. Let not your heart be troubled, neither let it be afraid." (John 14:27)

In Mark 5:30, look at how Jesus responds to the woman who had just touched Him. Her faith gave her away!

"And Jesus, immediately knowing in himself that virtue had gone out of him, turned him about in the press, and said, Who touched my clothes?"

With all the people pushing and shoving, Peter, Christ's disciple, couldn't figure out how Jesus could ask such a question. Everyone was touching Him (Luke 8:45). But Jesus felt a *special* touch, one different from any other. He literally felt His power leave His body, and He immediately knew that someone had touched Him with absolute faith. Remember, the woman had said, "If I may touch but his clothes, I shall be whole." That was great faith within itself because she did not have to physically touch Christ's body to receive her healing. His garment was enough.

Now that she had touched Jesus and He had asked aloud who touched Him, the woman had to reveal herself to Him and to everyone else. She must've been trembling with fear. By Jewish law, she was unclean. Therefore, she could have been killed for touching a rabbi and making Him unclean, or for being in the crowd and making everyone else unclean. But look at the love of Jesus! He never deviated from His mission—the one so beautifully stated in Luke 4:18-19. "The Spirit of the Lord is upon me, because he has anointed me to proclaim good news to the poor. He has sent me to proclaim liberty to the captives and recovering of sight to the blind, to set at liberty those who are oppressed, to proclaim the year of the Lord's favor." (ESV)

Jesus set the woman free from *all* of her issues—not just the bleeding, but of being the outcast, of her loneliness, desperation, and fear, and of her lack of family and all the torment that came with it. All of these issues were debilitating to her life, yet Christ had her come out into the open for everyone to see because she no longer had to live in hiding. How did she respond?

"The woman fearing and trembling, knowing what was done in her, came and fell down before him, and told him all the truth. And he said unto her, Daughter, thy faith hath made thee whole; go in peace, and be whole." (Mark 5:33-34).

Did you see that? Jesus called her "daughter." He let her know that she now had a family. She was part of the holy family of God. Everyone knew that she was accepted and that she was one of His. When He said "daughter," she was set fully *free*—and she could go on living in strength and with her head held high.

How amazing it is that Jesus knows exactly what is needed for our lives. He knows what will set us free to live in peace and victory. The Spirit is leading me to pray for all of us as women. Agree with me.

"Father in Heaven, the Father who loves His daughters unconditionally; the Father who has shown His love for woman since before creation. I come before you on behalf of my sisters all over the world. I pray for every woman who may be dealing with an issue within or external. Lord, I know you have the power to heal us. Help us with our unbelief so we will bring our issues to you, knowing without a shadow of a doubt that you will heal us. Thank you for loving us with an eternal love and for accepting us right where we are. Let this be a new beginning of drawing closer to you, and seeing ourselves as you see us, so we may be a blessing to the Kingdom of God and to you. Amen."

THE ISSUE OF JEALOUSY: MIRIAM

Miriam, the sister of Moses, was a woman who was given great influence and faith by God at an early age. We first meet her in Exodus 2 as her infant brother is sent down the river Nile in a basket in a desperate effort to save him from the Pharaoh's edict to kill all Hebrew baby boys. "And his sister stood at a distance to know what would be done to him." (Exodus 2:4, ESV) Miriam, a Hebrew slave, showed great bravery in doing this, but what happened next took even more courage.

> "Now the daughter of Pharaoh came down to bathe at the river, while her young women walked beside the river. She saw the basket among the reeds and sent her servant woman, and she took it. When she opened it, she saw the child, and behold, the baby was crying. She took pity on him and said, 'This is one of the Hebrews' children.' Then his sister said to Pharaoh's daughter, 'Shall I go and call you a nurse from the Hebrew women to nurse the child for you?' And Pharaoh's daughter said to her, 'Go.' So the girl went and called the child's mother." (Exodus 2:5-8, ESV)

Miriam knew about Pharaoh's decree, and she understood that it was not her place to address the princess of Egypt. But Miriam also realized that she needed to ensure her brother was cared for by his mother, Jochebed. What wisdom from a young girl! Miriam's actions proved vital to the salvation of the eventual deliverer of the Hebrew people.

The next time we see Miriam is right after the splitting of the Red Sea when God saved the Israelites from Pharaoh's army. This time, the Bible gives her a title: Miriam the prophetess, and she is portrayed as leading the women of Israel in praise to the Lord. "Then Miriam the prophetess, the sister of Aaron, took a tambourine in her hand, and all the women went out after her with tambourines and dancing. And Miriam sang to them: 'Sing to the Lord, for he has triumphed gloriously; the horse and his rider he has thrown into the sea.'" (Exodus 15:20-21, ESV) Although Moses had started the song of praise, Miriam boldly and confidently broke out in song and in great jubilee after seeing the astounding, saving power of God.

She and all the women danced in freedom, just as we should whenever we remember what Christ did to give us freedom by conquering sin and death through His sacrifice on the cross. Note that Miriam did not need to gain permission to do what she did, which validated her position as a leader among the people. Speaking on God's behalf, Micah said, "I brought you up out of Egypt and redeemed you from the land of slavery. I sent Moses to lead you, also Aaron and Miriam." (Micah 6:4, NIV) Miriam is recognized as the very first prophetess in the Bible, and according to Herbert Lockyer in *All the Women of the Bible*, "Prophetesses are those raised up by God and inspired by His Spirit to proclaim the will and purpose of God."

Miriam carried out her calling throughout her life, and although the name Miriam means "bitter" in Arabic, and many Hebrew personalities were associated by the meaning of their name, God saw all of Miriam's qualities and abilities. She was loved by all of Israel, and she loved the people, too. Her life was committed to God and to them.

But Miriam had issues with envy and prejudice. Later, when Moses married a Cushite (Ethiopian) woman, a woman of color, Miriam took offense to that, and the situation revealed her jealousy toward her brother.

"Miriam and Aaron talked against Moses behind his back because of his Cushite wife (he had married a Cushite woman). They said, 'Is it only through Moses that God speaks? Doesn't he also speak through us?' God overheard their talk." (Numbers 12:1-2, MSG)

Indeed, God did hear them—but how did He respond? Prejudice is to prejudge. Racism is hatred of someone who is different. Miriam may have likely been more prejudging the Cushite woman than hating her, but we don't know for sure. What we do know is that she had a problem with her brother's choice to marry her, and jealousy was the catalyst that revealed her issue. Her prejudice and envy were tied together—and the Lord's response addressed both at the same time.

"God broke in suddenly on Moses and Aaron and Miriam saying, 'Come out, you three, to the Tent of Meeting.' The three went out. God descended in a Pillar of Cloud and stood at the entrance to the Tent. He called Aaron and Miriam to him. When they stepped out, he said, Listen carefully to what I'm telling you. If there is a prophet of God among you, I make myself known to him in visions, I speak to him in dreams. But I don't do it that way with my servant Moses; he has the run of my entire house; I speak to him intimately, in person, in plain talk without riddles: He ponders the very form of God. So why did you show no reverence or respect in speaking against my servant, against Moses? The anger of God blazed out against them. And then he left. When the Cloud moved off from the Tent, oh! Miriam had turned leprous, her skin like snow. Aaron took one look at Miriam—a leper!" (Numbers 12:4-10, MSG)

Miriam was jealous of the authority Moses had over all of Israel, and she was envious of the position God had given him, despite the fact that God had also made her both a leader and a prophetess. Did she resent the fact that he was her younger brother? Did she feel that he could do anything he wanted, including marrying someone other than an Israelite? Did she believe he should have asked for her blessing first before marrying the Ethiopian woman? The Bible is silent on these questions, but the way God responded showed that the Lord was very serious about how Miriam was trying to cause insurrection against her brother's authority. His punishment was immediate and severe.

The fact that God called Miriam and Aaron to the Tent of Meeting was also significant. That location was outside the camp and was where the Lord rested His spirit upon the elders of the people, causing them to prophesy (Numbers 11:24-25). It was also designated as the place where God could talk to Moses and reveal His glory. Whenever God needed to communicate something of importance for the people, He called Moses out of the camp and into the tent. Therefore, for God to call both Aaron and Miriam to the tent with Moses showed the seriousness of what He had to say.

In verses 6-8, the Lord told them how he spoke to Moses face to face, meaning He had an intimate relationship with him, and He said that Moses had the first and last say over the Israelite people. God made it clear to Aaron and Miriam that when they spoke against the man that represented Him, it was the same as speaking against God Himself. Everything Moses did was under the Lord's direction. In addition, God was communicating that there cannot be division among His chosen leaders because those leaders are to be a representation of how God wants everyone else to conduct themselves.

Church leaders today—particularly pastors, deacons, elders, and teachers—let me be clear. There is *no* room in God's Kingdom purposes for division, jealousy, or prejudice among you. The Lord says you must be in unity and serve one another with love, mutual respect, and understanding. Those under your leadership do so trusting that God has chosen you and speaks directly to them through you. If, as leaders, you engage in division, envy, or prejudice, the rest of the congregation will follow your poor example. No wonder James 3:14-16 says, "But if you harbor bitter envy and selfish ambition in your hearts, do not boast about it or deny the truth. Such 'wisdom' does not come down from heaven but is earthly, unspiritual, demonic. For where you have envy and selfish ambition, there you find disorder and every evil practice." (NIV)

> *There is no room in God's Kingdom purposes for division, jealousy, or prejudice.*

As women of substance, we must strive to be examples to our fellow believers, showing the love of God in every situation and for all people. This requires us to look deeply within and examine ourselves to see if we have issues like Miriam's. Ask yourself, "Do I have envy, strife, or bitterness?" "Do I struggle with anger, malice, prejudice, or hatred toward others?" "Am I willing to take these things to the Lord and acknowledge that they exist within me?"

Miriam was a great woman who was chosen by God, but she had issues that she should have addressed herself, before God had to do it for her. Miriam's example shows us that we need to address our own issues before God has to step in. The Lord wants us to truthfully admit our faults, and He will be faithful to help us with them.

Though Miriam's punishment was leprosy, look at the love and humility of Moses. In Numbers 12:13, he prayed and asked God to heal her, the very one who was gossiping about him and trying to cause division among the people. This is an example of a true leader—just like Jesus on the cross when He said of those crucifying Him, "Father, forgive them, for they do not know what they are doing." (Luke 23:34, NIV) While we may have specific spiritual gifts and callings from the Lord, we are still human and have to admit that we are imperfect and are in need of God's help.

The rest of Numbers 12 reveals what happened next. Miriam was sent outside the Israelite camp for seven days before she was allowed back in. So, by the time that week was finished, Miriam had been healed of her leprosy. Otherwise, she would not have been able to return. Numbers 20:1 briefly mentions Miriam's death, but her legacy of being a woman of substance who had great influence and faith remains with us.

THE ISSUE OF BEING VICTIMIZED: TAMAR

As women, we have suffered severely from sins that have been committed against us. Some of those sins can rightly be viewed as desecrations. There is one woman in the Bible whose story is rarely mentioned from the pulpit or in the classroom, but I want to spotlight her because she was a victim of one of the greatest sins of desecration: rape.

Her name is Tamar, and her tragic story is told in 2 Samuel 13. Tamar was the daughter of King David, sister of Absalom and half-sister to Amnon. The Bible tells us that Tamar was a beautiful virgin princess who wore a colorful cloak that symbolized her purity. Unfortunately, Amnon lusted after Tamar. His indecent passion was so vile that it literally made him ill. Once Amnon settled in his heart to defile his sister, he had to set a trap to get her to come to his chambers. That was necessary because it was customary for virgin princesses to live in a quarters separated from all of the men to protect their honor. Therefore, Amnon needed Tamar to be away from her safe place so that he could violate her.

After telling his advisor he was "in love" with Tamar (2 Samuel 13:4), Amnon was encouraged to pretend to be sick, and then ask his father, David, to have Tamar come to him and prepare food for him. Amnon did just that, and David responded accordingly.

What a terrible shame. At that moment, David not only compromised his rule over Israel to appease the son who was heir apparent to the throne, but he needlessly compromised his daughter's safety. Why would Amnon need his sister to make food for him? He had servants who could take care of that. Yet David did not see Amnon's request as strange. When Tamar arrived, at her father's request, to serve Amnon, her half-brother instructed her to cook for him. He then sent away all the servants so the two of them would be alone. Once the food was prepared, Amnon asked Tamar to come into his bedroom to feed it to him.

When she was close enough, Amnon grabbed her and demanded that she come to bed with him. A terrified Tamar showed incredible wisdom and inner strength by trying to reason with her attacker.

> "'No, brother!' she said, 'Don't hurt me! This kind of thing isn't done in Israel! Don't do this terrible thing! Where could I ever show my face? And you—you'll be out on the street in disgrace. Oh, please! Speak to the king—he'll let you marry me.' But he wouldn't listen. Being much stronger than she, he raped her." (2 Samuel 13:12-14, MSG)

Can you imagine the horrific scene? Even as she was being attacked, Tamar attempted in desperation to remind her half-brother of God's law, appealing to his heart to recognize that what he was doing was wrong. But Amnon had no heart. He was beyond reproach. Next, Tamar attempted to appeal to Amnon's empathy for her, but he was beyond humane. Finally, she tried to convince him to ask the king for her hand in marriage, even though she knew that was forbidden. It was her last-ditch hope, but it was to no avail.

So, what was Tamar's issue here? She was victimized. Any man who rapes a woman is the one with the issue. He is the detestable one, not the woman—and in the case of Amnon, God's law was clearly against him. "Don't have sex with your sister, whether she's your father's daughter or your mother's, whether she was born in the same house or elsewhere." (Leviticus 18:9, MSG) Such sexual sin was seen by God as wicked (Leviticus 18:17). Deuteronomy 22:25-27 (MSG) added, "But if it was out in the country that the man found the engaged girl and grabbed and raped her, only the man is to die, the man who raped her. Don't do anything to the girl; she did nothing wrong. This is similar to the case of a man who comes across his neighbor out in the country and murders him; when the engaged girl yelled out for help, there was no one around to hear or help her." It's significant how God compares rape to killing. Rape is just like murdering someone.

Amnon had no excuse and no justification, and Tamar had done nothing wrong. But Amnon was beyond seeing reason. His lust became wickedness, and that wickedness birthed loathing.

"No sooner had Amnon raped her than he hated her—an immense hatred. The hatred that he felt for her was greater than the love he'd had for her. 'Get up,' he said, 'and get out!' 'Oh no, brother,' she said. 'Please! This is an even worse evil than what you just did to me!' But he wouldn't listen to her. He called for his valet. 'Get rid of this woman. Get her out of my sight! And lock the door after her.' The valet threw her out and locked the door behind her. She was wearing a long-sleeved gown. (That's how virgin princesses used to dress from early adolescence on.) Tamar poured ashes on her head, then she ripped the long-sleeved gown, held her head in her hands, and walked away, sobbing as she went." (2 Samuel 13:15-19, MSG)

Look at how Amnon treated Tamar after the rape. His so-called love instantly transformed to hate, which shows that Amnon never truly loved her in the first place. Not only was Amnon consumed with lust, but he exhibited the characteristics of a sociopath. He had Tamar thrown out of his chambers as though she was garbage, and he had the door locked behind her so that she could not re-enter. Incredibly, Tamar even tried to reason with Amnon again, insisting that throwing her out was worse than the rape itself. In Jewish culture, only a virgin could be betrothed to a man, so she reasoned it would have been better for her to stay with her rapist and live as his wife than to be an outcast with her innocence stolen, her future of becoming a bride confiscated, and being looked upon by others as nothing more than spoiled goods assured.

But Amnon discarded her anyway.

Tamar was annihilated by this act of violence. She left weeping, and she tore the cloak that she wore as a demonstration of her now-stolen purity. Tamar was utterly destroyed physically and emotionally. What once was joy was now misery. Where once was hope of a bright future was now hopelessness. Where once was life was now death.

When her brother, Absalom, found out what happened, he took her into his home and told her not to say a word about the rape (2 Samuel 13:20). Though Absalom began plotting to kill Amnon as revenge, he did not minister to Tamar. She was left with no emotional help. Even when her father, David, learned of the rape, there was no comfort given to Tamar and no repercussion to Amnon for his abhorrent actions. "Tamar lived in her brother Absalom's house, a desolate woman. King David heard the whole story and was enraged, but he didn't discipline Amnon. David doted on him because he was his firstborn. Absalom quit speaking to Amnon—not a word, whether good or bad—because he hated him for violating his sister Tamar." (2 Samuel 13:20-22, MSG)

In Phyllis Trible's book, *Texts of Terror*, she wrote this about desolation. "When used of people elsewhere in scripture, the verb *be desolate* connotes being destroyed by an enemy … or being torn to pieces by an animal." Tamar was a princess, but her status did not prevent her rape. She did not receive the help she needed. Tamar lived out her life in a state of mental anguish and emotional destitution.

Where was the justice for Tamar? Where was David's devotion to Tamar? Both were non-existent. The entire incident was dismissed. Ultimately, Absalom carried out God's law and killed Amnon for raping his sister, preventing Amnon from possessing the throne of Israel—but did any of that help Tamar? It did not. Although Absalom named one of his daughters after her, nothing else is said of Tamar in Scripture.

Dear daughter of the Most High King, you do not have to end up like Tamar. If you have been raped and have not yet sought help, please do so immediately. Look within your inner circle of friends or family for the support you need from those who will listen to you and empathize with you. Do not hesitate to seek professional therapeutic help. Lean on the Lord and the Word of God for peace. You can recover from this violent crime, and God is ready and willing to heal you. The Lord has compassion for your soul, and as you turn to Him for comfort, He *will* be there for you. God's Word has stated that you are not to blame, so do not blame yourself. You are worthy of love—most of all, God's love.

Lean on the Lord and the Word of God for peace.

In Joyce Meyer's book, *Battlefield of the Mind: Winning the Battle in Your Mind*, she wrote, "When a person is going through a hard time, his mind wants to give up. Satan knows that if he can defeat us in our mind, he can defeat us in our experience. That's why it is so important that we not lose heart, grow weary, and faint." God our Father will fortify you. He is the one who created you with strong substance to overcome any adversity in your life. Operate in the strength the Lord has placed within you, living out Paul's exhortation. "Therefore, put on every piece of God's armor so you will be able to resist the enemy in the time of evil. Then after the battle you will still be standing firm." (Ephesians 6:13, NLT)

Hold your head up, and know that the Lord is God, and you are His daughter. Allow me to pray. "Father in Heaven, I lift my heart to you on behalf of all your daughters who have suffered from the violent act of rape. Father, I ask you to heal the brokenness, bitterness, and desolation. Mend those who are suffering silently and alone. Send someone to minister to their pain with compassion and empathy. Make them new within their souls, fill them with joy, and give them a new outlook on life, filled with purpose and destiny. In the mighty name of Jesus. Amen."

A WOMAN OF EVIL SUBSTANCE: JEZEBEL

In addition to those who dealt with specific issues, the Bible also tells us about women who fully used their substance against God's purposes for evil—determined to gain power and prestige by any means necessary.

One such woman was Jezebel, infamous for her wicked, seductive, idolatrous, murderous, lying, and selfish character. We are first introduced to her in 1 Kings 16:30-32 as the wife of Ahab, the king of Israel. He did evil in the sight of God, so it was appropriate for him to have a wife who was just like him, but Jezebel was worse. She did not worship the one true God but came from a family and a country that worshipped idol gods such as Baal and Ashtaroth, to whom were attributed fertility, rain, and prosperity. Baal was the male sun god to whom people made human sacrifices, while Astaroth was the female god thought of as a reflection of Baal.

Jezebel's marriage to the king of Israel could have presented an opportunity for her to know the true and living God, but because Ahab was wicked and did not follow the commandments of God, that did not happen.

Jezebel's evil character was revealed in a conversation between God's prophet, Elijah, and Obadiah, Ahab's palace administrator, in 1 Kings 18:1-15. Obadiah explained to Elijah that when Jezebel tried to kill all the prophets of Israel, he was able to save 100 prophets of the Lord from her by secretly hiding them in caves and supplying them with the food and water they needed to survive. Jezebel had erected her own temple of worship to her idol gods and placed 400 of her own prophets of Baal within the temple. She had also selected another 450 prophets to serve in the temple her husband, Ahab, had built in Samaria. Jezebel's intention was nothing less than to wipe out any trace of the true God and put the god, Baal, in His place. She ruled with complete contempt for the Lord and all that He represented. Murder was in her heart, and she did not hesitate to commit it.

The next time we hear about Jezebel is when she threatened Elijah after the great prophet of God had successfully challenged the prophets of Baal and proven that their god was no match for the Lord. The prophets of Baal were destroyed, and God was shown to be the most powerful (1 Kings 18:20-40). Yet this made Jezebel furious, and she directed her wrath at Elijah.

"Ahab reported to Jezebel everything that Elijah had done, including the massacre of the prophets. Jezebel immediately sent a messenger to Elijah with her threat: 'The gods will get you for this and I'll get even with you! By this time tomorrow you'll be as dead as any one of those prophets.' When Elijah saw how things were, he ran for dear life to Beersheba, far in the south of Judah. He left his young

161

servant there and then went on into the desert another day's journey." (1 Kings 19:1-3, MSG)

What? Elijah had just exhibited the power and might of the Lord God of Israel to the people and destroyed the prophets of Baal. But look at this woman's powerful influence! When Elijah got Jezebel's message, he became scared and ran away. His fear became so great he even begged God to take his life (1 Kings 19:4). Elijah knew Baal did not have any power against God, and he had no fear of the king, but Jezebel? She was that frightening! Elijah had performed an amazing miracle, yet he chillingly feared her. Jezebel had a treacherous reputation because of her evil and violent behavior. If Elijah, who talked and walked with God, was afraid of her, the rest of the nation did not stand a chance.

We all have a choice—and as women, we can use our God-given substance for good or for evil. When we decide to live in a way that is contrary to God, we show our true character and our sinful nature, and we set ourselves up to lose our relationship with our Savior. We were created in His image to be a reflection of Him, so when we do not reveal the image of God through our lives, we place ourselves in opposition to our intended purpose. We are strong and destined for greatness in the Lord. We are to do good and not evil.

As women, we can use our God-given substance for good or for evil.

When we seek to devour others through our thoughts, actions, or words, we take on the characteristics of Satan himself. He goes constantly throughout the earth (Job 1:7) "as a roaring lion ... seeking whom he may devour." (1 Peter 5:8) This has been the devil's intention from the very beginning. His purpose is to try to destroy us or lead us away from the Lord so that we won't see or feel the wonderful presence of our merciful God. When we live to do evil, we miss out on so much that God has for us—most of all, His presence, peace, and provision. But praise the Lord, Jesus said, "a thief is only there to steal and kill and destroy. I came so they can have real and eternal life, more and better life than they ever dreamed of." (John 10:10, MSG)

Our strength and substance as women is to declare *His* glory and to show others the immeasurable, loving nature of God. If you know there are some evil issues in your life that need to change, you can do that through Jesus Christ. Just repent, make an about face, and walk away from those behaviors. Then ask God to forgive you, and please make sure to forgive yourself as well. From then on, walk in the Spirit of the Lord, following the instructions of the Bible to "stand fast therefore in the liberty wherewith Christ hath made us free, and be not entangled again with the yoke of bondage." (Galatians 5:1) Surrendering your life to Christ is to live according to the Word of God with intention. His Holy Spirit will fortify you to carry out your destiny in God! Just as Joshua did, choose *this day* who you will serve. (Joshua 24:14-15)

Elijah had fled into the wilderness, but God met him there and sent angels to minister to him, feeding and protecting him before giving Elijah instructions about his next assignment (1 Kings 19:5-18). Jezebel's threat against the prophet of God did not come to fruition. In the end, Elijah had absolutely nothing to worry about. Remember, no matter what anyone has planned or plotted against you, it will not prosper. Their weapons may form, but they will not prevent what God has decreed in your abundant life. Do not fear or fret. Just trust in the God you serve, and He will direct your path.

As for Jezebel, she kept going. The next time we see her, in 1 Kings 21, Jezebel is actually taking on the role of the king by sentencing a man to his death. Naboth, a vineyard owner, had turned down an offer to have his land purchased by King Ahab. A man who feared God, Naboth instead wanted to keep the land within his family in adherence to the laws of God (Leviticus 25:23-24). Ahab knew the law, but he was still distraught that Naboth would not sell him the land, so the petulant king went home and began to sulk. When Jezebel saw her husband acting the way he was, she wasn't going to have it.

> "Is this how you act as king over Israel? Get up and eat! Cheer up. I'll get you the vineyard of Naboth the Jezreelite." (1 Kings 21:7)

She put her evil plan into action. First, she contacted the leaders of Jezreel by letter, using the king's seal and calling for a fast in the name of God. We know, of course, that this was not done from the heart. Jezebel despised the God of Israel. Yet she was so malicious, she used Israel's reverence for the Lord to set a trap for Naboth. Next, Jezebel hired two men called the sons of Belial (in Hebrew, Belial means worthless, ungodly, or wicked) to accuse Naboth of blaspheming against God and the king. Jezebel was easily able to persuade these men to do evil, conspire with her, and lie in wait to kill Naboth. They feared her more than God Himself.

Jezebel knew enough about Jewish culture to know the men would be able to stone Naboth to death under the law of two witnesses to accuse someone of a crime (Deuteronomy 17:6-7)—in this case, blasphemy against God and king. Naboth was taken outside of the city and stoned. Commandments of covetousness, bearing false witness, stealing, murder, and using God's name in vain were all broken in just this one act, yet Jezebel did it to seize land that did not belong to her or Ahab. Even worse, she did it all in the name of the Lord.

After making sure an innocent man was killed to appease her husband, Jezebel informed Ahab that he could obtain the land because Naboth was dead, and he wasted no time in doing so.

There was nothing Jezebel would not do to get what she wanted. It's clear why 1 Kings 21:25 states of Ahab, "But there was none like unto Ahab, which did sell himself to work wickedness in the sight of the Lord, whom Jezebel his wife stirred up." There was no end to Jezebel's ability to stir up evil.

But there was an end to God's tolerance. The Lord became fed up with both her and her husband, and He spoke to Elijah to tell them that their time to cause the children of Israel to sin against Him and do evil in the land was just about over.

> "But the Lord said to Elijah, 'Go down to meet King Ahab of Israel, who rules in Samaria. He will be at Naboth's vineyard in Jezreel, claiming it for himself. Give him this message: "This is what the Lord says: Wasn't it enough that you killed Naboth? Must you rob him, too? Because you have done this, dogs will lick your blood at the very place where they licked the blood of Naboth!"' 'So, my enemy, you have found me!' Ahab exclaimed to Elijah. 'Yes,' Elijah answered, 'I have come because you have sold yourself to what is evil in the Lord's sight. So now the Lord says, "I will bring disaster on you and consume you. I will destroy every one of your male descendants, slave and free alike, anywhere in Israel! I am going to destroy your family as I did the family of Jeroboam son of Nebat and the family of Baasha son of Ahijah, for you have made me very angry and have led Israel into sin."' And regarding Jezebel, the Lord says, "Dogs will eat Jezebel's body at the plot of land in Jezreel."' (1 Kings 21:17-21, NLT)

Interestingly, when Ahab heard the prophesy from Elijah, he humbled himself and repented to the Lord. He fasted and prayed, and God had mercy on him (1 Kings 21:27-29). God is a God of second chances! But after three years, Ahab returned to serving idol gods and doing evil. So, God called Elijah to put an end to the wickedness of Ahab, anointing Jehu King of Israel and giving him an assignment: to kill the household of Ahab, including Jezebel (2 Kings 9:7-10). When Jezebel realized her time was up, she arrogantly put make up on her face and clothed herself so that she would die as a queen with dignity and honor. But that would not stop the word of the Lord from coming to pass.

"In the eleventh year of the reign of Joram son of Ahab, Ahaziah had become king of Judah. When Jezebel heard that Jehu had arrived in Jezreel, she made herself up—put on eyeshadow and arranged her hair—and posed seductively at the window. When Jehu came through the city gate, she called down, 'So, how are things, 'Zimri,' you dashing king-killer?' Jehu looked up at the window and called, 'Is there anybody up there on my side?' Two or three palace eunuchs looked out. He ordered, 'Throw her down!' They threw her out the window. Her blood spattered the wall and the horses, and Jehu trampled her under his horse's hooves. Then Jehu went inside and ate his lunch. During lunch he gave orders, 'Take care of that damned woman; give her a decent burial—she is, after all, a king's daughter.' They went out to bury her, but there was nothing left of her but skull, feet, and hands. They came back and told Jehu. He said, 'It's God's word, the word spoken by Elijah the Tishbite: In the field of Jezreel, dogs will eat Jezebel; The body of Jezebel will be like dog-droppings on the ground in Jezreel. Old friends and lovers will say, 'I wonder, is this Jezebel?'" (2 Kings 9:29-37, MSG)

Both Ahab and Jezebel died exactly as the prophesy decreed. They also left behind a legacy of evil (2 Chronicles 21:1-6), which was passed on from generation to generation. In fact, when their own daughter, Athaliah, became queen of Judah, she initiated the worship of Baal and helped to plan the murder of all of her husband's siblings so that, after her husband died, her son would become king. She also did not hesitate to kill her own grandchildren to secure the throne for herself (2 Kings 11:1-20, 2 Chronicles 22:10-12). Nothing good ever comes out of doing evil.

Daughter of the King, do all that you can to live the life Christ has died for you to have—

one of abundance. My father had a saying, "Do all the good you can do, and then stop! Say all the good you can say, and then hush!" As usual, my daddy was right. Trust in your Heavenly Father today.

A WOMAN OF GODLY SUBSTANCE: HULDAH

In stark contrast to Jezebel was a powerful woman who used her gifts from God and strength for serving God to proclaim His Word in a time when the entire nation of Judah was lost in a quagmire of idolatry and sin. They had lost the Book of the Law and were living a life of degradation before God in Heaven—but Huldah, a prophetess of the Lord, walked with God in the midst of it all.

Huldah lived in the center of the city of Jerusalem, and she was willing and ready to advise anyone who came to her. She was married to Shallum, a keeper of King Josiah's wardrobe. Josiah was the sixteenth king of Judah and ruled long after Ahab and Jezebel had controlled Israel, yet the two nations were intertwined both through military strategy and through intermarriage with the daughters of foreign nations to maintain peace between Judah, Israel, and the nations around them. Still, by Huldah's time, both Judah and Israel were worshipping idol gods and living in disobedience to the Lord. Josiah began his reign at the age of eight, and fortunately, he desired to implement righteousness in Judah and reinstate worship of the one, true God among the people. When the Book of the Law was discovered during repairs in the Temple at Jerusalem, what happened next was significant.

"It came to pass, when the king had heard the words of the book of the law, that he rent his clothes. And the king commanded Hilkiah the priest, and Ahikam the son of Shaphan, and Achbor the son of Michaiah, and Shaphan the scribe, and Asahiah a servant of the king's, saying, Go ye, enquire of the Lord for me, and for the people, and for all Judah, concerning the words of this book that is found: for great is the wrath of the Lord that is kindled against us, because our fathers have not hearkened unto the words of this book, to do according unto all that which is written concerning us. So Hilkiah the priest, and Ahikam, and Achbor, and Shaphan, and Asahiah, went unto Huldah the prophetess, the wife of Shallum the son of Tikvah, the son of Harhas, keeper of the wardrobe; (now she dwelt in Jerusalem in the college;) and they communed with her." (2 Kings 22:11-14)

Jeremiah was a great prophet at that time, but notice that Hilkiah, and his entourage from King Josiah, did not call upon him, but on Huldah. She must have had an exceptional reputation for prophesying what the Lord had spoken. What did Huldah tell them?

"Thus saith the Lord, Behold, I will bring evil upon this place, and upon the inhabitants thereof, even all the words of the book which the king of Judah hath read: Because they have forsaken me, and have burned incense unto other gods, that they might provoke me to anger with all the works of their hands; therefore my wrath shall be kindled against this place, and shall not be quenched." (2 Kings 22:16-17)

Without hesitation, Huldah boldly proclaimed what God had spoken about the rebellion of the people and how they would suffer because of their disobedience. Huldah's declaration from the Lord led the king and country to repent, change their ways, and give reverence to Almighty God.

Look at how one woman played a major role in changing the trajectory of an entire nation. Even more impressive is the fact that Hilkiah the priest sought a woman for the answer from God. Huldah was highly regarded for her prophetic gift and her commitment to the Lord. The king and the high priest trusted her discernment and acted upon it. The rest of 2 Kings 22 tells how and why the Lord decided not to pour out His wrath.

God will speak through us, and something good always happens when we stand up for the Lord.

How did Huldah stay dedicated to the Lord when everyone else had turned away? Scripture doesn't tell us—but the lesson is clear. Your faith in God as His daughter is an individual faith. No matter what others are saying and doing that is contrary to the Lord, you can remain committed to His truth and righteousness. Huldah did, she was blessed, and the whole nation was saved because of her faithfulness to God. In *All of the Women of the Bible*, Edith Deen wrote, "Noteworthy it is that in the short account of Huldah's prophecy the scribe repeated four times her phrase, 'Thus saith the Lord,' making us know that Huldah did not think of herself as an oracle, but only as a channel through which God's word came."

So it is with us as women of substance. We are important to God, and we have divine purpose from Him. God will speak through us, and something good always happens when we stand up for the Lord. Do not be afraid or embarrassed. Instead, "trust in the Lord with all thine heart; and lean not unto thine own understanding. In all thy ways acknowledge him, and he shall direct thy paths." (Proverbs 3:5-6)

Jezebel used her strength for evil. Huldah used her strength for good. One led a nation into rebellion; the other led a nation to repentance. What kind of woman will you be? You have a choice. Like Huldah, be a woman of godly substance.

PART FOUR

Let Your Substance Grow!

Chapter 10

"After this, Jesus knowing that all things were now accomplished, that the scripture might be fulfilled, saith, I thirst."
(John 19:28)

Our relationship with Jesus Christ must be ongoing and never ending. We must commune with Him daily, continuing to have an unquenchable desire for His presence.

The last message Jesus left for us on the cross, recorded in John 19:28, provides our catalyst to do this and stay hydrated for God.

"I thirst."

Spoken during His crucifixion after He had experienced hours of brutal torture in the hot sun, Jesus—with a crown of thorns on His head and nails piercing His hands and feet—knew that everything necessary to secure the salvation of our souls had been accomplished.

Yet in these two words, knowing that death was upon Him, Christ still requested water from His abusers. Why?

To be thirsty is a reminder that something is missing from our physical bodies. Up to 60 percent of the human body is made up of water; the brain and heart each consist of nearly 75 percent water, and the lungs are over 80 percent water.[1] Water is essential for life: it is a cleansing agent, it transports nutrients to our bodies through our blood, and it regulates body temperature through sweat when our bodies become overheated. Humans cannot live more than three days without water consumption.[2] It's no accident that God created the Earth with most of its surface covered with water. He knew we need water to exist, and thirst expresses the desire for that need.

In the same way, we cannot survive spiritually without the Holy Spirit. We cannot commune with God and become one with Him without the Spirit. We need the Spirit to maintain our connection with the Lord. The Holy Spirit transports us into another spiritual realm, transforming us into new creatures in Christ. The Spirit produces eternal life and helps us discern what God is saying to us. It regulates our relationship with God the Father and prevents us from becoming stagnant in that relationship. In short, the Holy Spirit is the nutrient for our souls and the life agent of our spiritual lives, eliminating the issues of our sin by constantly cleansing us from them.

> *We cannot commune with God and become one with Him without the Spirit.*

But there is an additional application of Christ's declaration in John 19:28—and it is found earlier in that same Gospel in the story of the woman at the well. In Chapter 3, you'll recall that we learned how the account of the woman at the well in John 4 teaches us to be strong and to fortify our strength through worship so that we can have a loving relationship with God that encompasses reverence and obedience to Him. But that story also serves to provide vital contrasts and parallels between physical water and spiritual water.

In John 4, Christ uses His request for physical water to provide a parallel to the eternal water of the Holy Spirit. "Jesus answered and said unto her, Whosoever drinketh of this water shall thirst again: But whosoever drinketh of the water that I shall give him shall never thirst; but the water that I shall give him shall be in him a well of water springing up into everlasting life." (John 4:13-14) This always reminds me of the Calistoga Geyser, the "Old Faithful Geyser of California" in Napa County. It is a natural phenomenon located in a picturesque setting of green mountains and hills. When my husband and I visited the geyser, I was amazed at how it erupted every few minutes. I thought to myself, *This is what Jesus was talking about with the woman at the well. The living water of the Holy Spirit is continual into eternity.* (See Revelation 21:6 for a reference to this eternal water of the Spirit.)

Christ's words in John 4 peaked the woman's interest because He knew she was thirsty in her soul. She did not understand that she was missing a spiritual relationship with God, though she thought she had one. That encounter was so special because Jesus took the time to give the woman a new lease on life. Jesus helped her see that it was only through the Holy Spirit that she could become one with God. Christ was God, full of the Holy Spirit and explaining how the Spirit came through Him, yet also human enough to physically thirst and relate personally to the woman's situation and need for an intimate relationship with Him as Lord. In John 4, Jesus was spiritually filled and in total communion with His Father.

However, in John 19, Christ is both physically and spiritually depleted on the cross, showing His full humanity. As a man, He was thirsty for a drink, but as the Son of God, He was thirsty for the presence of God, to again be in communion and complete fellowship with Him as He always had been before. We are able to clearly see Christ as being both God and human even as His divine nature enabled Him to provide a way for us to be saved from our sins.

Earlier, when Jesus was praying in the Garden of Gethsemane, we can see further evidence of His divinity and humanity. "And he was withdrawn from them [some of His disciples] about a stone's cast, and kneeled down, and prayed, Saying, Father, if thou be willing, remove this cup from me: nevertheless not my will, but thine, be done." (Luke 22:41-42) As He prayed three different times to the Father to eliminate the cup of His coming death, the torture He was asking to be removed from was not the pain of the crucifixion itself. Rather, this passage explicitly reveals the anguish and torment Christ went through, knowing that He would be separated from the Father and not have the Holy Spirit with Him. It was agony for Jesus to not be in complete fellowship with the Father, yet He courageously resolved to do the will of His Father, no matter the cost.

Significantly, the crucifixion scene in John 19 was the only time Scripture records Jesus asking for water other than when He was with the woman at the well in John 4. That wasn't by accident. By emphasizing His own thirst on the cross, Jesus pointed us to our need to continually thirst for the Lord and His presence—and to how that thirst is quenched through the work of the Holy Spirit in our lives. Jesus doesn't want anyone to die without experiencing the new birth of the Holy Spirit. To do anything else is pure agony.

Ask yourself: "Am I thirsty in my soul?" "Is there an empty place in the center of my being?" If you answered "yes" to both questions, you can be filled with the Holy Spirit and discover a whole new way of thinking, speaking, and living. That was exactly what Jesus introduced to the woman in John 4 and what He reminded us to seek in John 19—a new life with God! But it only comes through accepting Jesus as your personal Savior, being born again in the Spirit (John 3:8), relinquishing control of your life to Christ, worshiping Him in Spirit and in truth (John 4:24), and making Him the love of your life. This is when you truly choose to follow the Word of God and live accordingly.

HOW DO I LET MY SUBSTANCE GROW?

Romans 10:9 declares, "If thou shalt confess with thy mouth the Lord Jesus, and shalt believe in thine heart that God hath raised him from the dead, thou shalt be saved." As a woman of substance, you must know and believe in your heart, soul, and mind that you are saved, valuable, and important to God. A woman of substance knows who she is and how God sees her—and it all starts with what you believe about yourself and your God.

Look in the mirror right now and ask yourself two questions. Be honest.

1. Am I utilizing the gifts within me, my very substance, to better the Kingdom of God, my family, my community, my church, and ultimately the world? I usually ask the Lord this question during my daily, intimate worship time with Him, and God always shows me something that I need to improve in my thinking, my speech, or my overall behavior to better utilize my gifts. I remember when God spoke to me about my gift of exhortation. He said the gift is the ability to encourage others to help bring out the best in them—it is a call to action. The Lord let me know that I have a gift to encourage others both with my words and through my love for Him. "Always have an encouraging and positive word for others," He told me, "and always speak out of love when correcting them. There is *power* in your words."

> *A woman of substance knows who she is and how God sees her.*

Then, the next time I was in worship experiencing my intimate time with the Lord, He whispered to me, "That same power that is in you to exhort others can have a powerfully harmful effect if you use it in a negative way." God counseled me to be careful of the spirit that was influencing my words because there is enough power in them to spiritually damage someone. He also told me to not allow anger or hurt feelings to influence my gift. Therefore, I make it a regular practice to check my feelings toward others and the spirit in which I am saying things to them.

2. Am I willing to change my unhealthy ways and thoughts so that they line up with the woman that God says I am? It all starts with having the will to change. There are some things I have no problem changing in my life, but there are others where I have to fast, pray, and ask God for His supernatural power to help me live out my substance as a woman. There is always room for correction and growth.

There was a time about five years into my relationship with the Lord that the Holy Spirit convicted me about my terrible habit of gossiping. My daily life was full of it, and it was so constant it had weaved itself into my Christian walk regardless of the fact that I was attending a Holy Ghost-filled church. I had established the behavior so well that I gossiped with everyone. The Holy Spirit stopped me in my tracks one day and let me see the consequences of gossip. He helped me understand how foul gossiping can be. The hurt and shame it placed upon others was very difficult to bear, not to mention the realization that I was one of the sources of this sin within my church. I did not notice how bad it was until God revealed it to me.

When I accepted that gossip was truly a method of emotional and spiritual *murder*, I was completely convicted. Still, it took me going completely silent for a while to get over it. I had to fast, pray, and learn how to properly talk to my friends and other Christians all over again. I am so glad I was able to overcome this terrible sin. I knew I could not be an exhorter and a gossip at the same time. The two are contrary to one another. God dealt with me because He was trying to bring out the gift of exhortation, and my sin of gossip was a hinderance to that.

Next, memorize and recite these Bible verses:

- Genesis 1:27—"So God created man in his own image, in the image of God created he him; male and female created he them." The Lord created men and women equal in His eyes, possessing the same Spirit to be equally used to further His Kingdom. A woman of substance moves and lives by the Holy Spirit and works cooperatively with men, even as we have different roles within the family.

- Psalm 139:14—"I will praise thee; for I am fearfully and wonderfully made: marvellous are thy works; and that my soul knoweth right well." This scripture affirms who we are and declares how strategically and purposefully the Lord designed us. We are awesome, wonderful, and marvelous women of God because the hand of God created us.

- Proverbs 31:30—"Favour is deceitful, and beauty is vain: but a woman that feareth the Lord, she shall be praised." A woman of substance places emphasis on her inward being, her character, and her heart for God and others, not upon her beauty or popularity. While it is important for women to keep and present themselves appropriately, this is not to be our focus. Rather, our lovely spirit will be praised without any prompting.

- Proverbs 31:10—"Who can find a virtuous woman? for her price is far above rubies." To be virtuous is to be a woman of moral excellence, someone who will not allow herself, her values, or her God to be compromised before others. It is *this* that establishes her worth.

- Proverbs 18:22—"Whoso findeth a wife findeth a good thing, and obtaineth favour of the Lord." A wife who loves the Lord is a blessing because her relationship with God brings favor to her husband. A woman of substance is incredibly valuable to herself, her family, and her community.

179

These scriptures are a constant reminder to help you hold your head up and be proud to be a woman of God. When you know who you are and Whose you are, you can begin to walk within your worth and right into your destiny.

Finally, follow these seven steps to *live* as a woman of substance.

1. Join and get involved in a healthy church. Ask your Christian friends or relatives for recommendations for a church where the pastor preaches and teaches the true Word of God and loves those who he is leading in such a way that it flows throughout the congregation. When you are in a loving environment where the members see each other as family, you can then begin your transformation to have more healthy and loving relationships in your life. A church must also be family oriented, having ministries for everyone in your home so they can grow emotionally and spiritually. Church members should be allowed to utilize their gifts to build up the ministry and the Kingdom of God to help the congregation grow spiritually. My church, for example, has a wonderful usher ministry where the head usher treats everyone special. She not only greets newcomers, but she also bakes a cake for everyone's birthday and sends them a card. I don't know how she does it, but her gift of hospitality demonstrates love within the church. Being a member of a healthy church will stimulate you to *grow* as a woman of substance and ensure that growth—but also remember there will always be differences and various personalities that may be difficult. Do not allow them to deter you.

When you know who you are and whose you are, you can begin to walk within your worth and right into your destiny.

2. Gain a good understanding of the Word of God. It is important that you learn how to live your daily life as a woman of substance through your knowledge of God's Word. As Proverbs

4:7 exhorts you, "Wisdom is the principal thing; therefore get wisdom: and with all thy getting get understanding." Be faithful to attend a weekly Bible study that gives you specific guidance and encouragement as a woman of God, and be sure to ask questions (no question is wrong). Until I began going to a Bible study, I did not know that God was looking for a loving relationship with me. I thought it was all about service, but I discovered instead that it is all about relationship. When you know God's Word, you will know what is expected of you by the Lord. You cannot live out what you do not know—and the Word of God is the *change agent* that guides you in your walk as a woman of substance.

3. Utilize your gifts to advance the Kingdom of God. This can be fulfilled in many ways, from cleaning the church building to assisting in a ministry at the church such as choir, children's ministry, hospitality, ministerial staff, pastor's aid, usher, or administrative duties. A great leader must first be a committed follower. Often as you give yourself over to ministry, you are *directed* to your gifts and to further training to become a leader. I started out singing in the choir. From there, I became a choir director, youth ministry leader, and a women's ministry leader to first lady of a church.

4. Connect with a like-minded female who encourages you to live for God. This person should make you better, propel you toward a more intimate relationship with the Lord, and encourage you to remain in Him. As a woman of substance, you should always be accountable to another woman. This strengthens you through *edification*, for as iron sharpens iron, one person sharpens another (Proverbs 27:17). This also gives you someone you can pray with and who will listen to you when you need an ear. Whenever I have a difficult decision to make and need a reminder to do the godly thing, I call on my sisters. They direct me toward the righteous way to handle the situation.

5. Fellowship with other ministries you are interested in. Fellowship is being with a community of people who share your interests, and going to women's conferences, workshops, and special services at various churches is a great way to fellowship with other women. Remember, though, to remain faithful first to the commitments you have made at your own church. As you fellowship with other women, you will have an opportunity to see God working in their lives, and that will *build up* your own faith. I teach a monthly women's Bible class in the community, and the women who attend come to hear and share God's Word and give insights on what the Lord has shown them. We have developed loving relationships between women from several different churches who have the same, common goals. They are my inspiration to keep going on in His name!

6. Maintain a devotional and worship time at home with God. Set aside time every day to read your Bible, worship, and pray to God. This can be anywhere from 15 minutes to one hour, and it is to be fully dedicated to the Lord to enhance your relationship with Him. Be sure to choose a place where you will not be interrupted, understanding that having worship time with God is the most important thing you can do as a woman of substance. It's when you *receive* from God alone. It is the purest experience you can have with the Lord. It is when you hear from Him and are intimately strengthened by the Holy Spirit. The more time you spend privately with God, the stronger your substance becomes as you are transformed into the woman God has created you to be. It was during my worship time that God revealed to me that I must write this book! It is a part of His purpose for my life!

7. Remain steadfast and immovable in your faith. When times get hard and difficult to endure, stay connected to Jesus Christ and your church. Seek help from those in your church family. *Allow* yourself time to be ministered to until you are strong enough to minister to others. Find rest in the Lord and never turn your back on God because He will never turn away from you. As Pastor Lorea Johnson of Friendly Will Baptist Church in Los Angeles, California, used to say, "Stay in the race."

GROWING MY SUBSTANCE IN OTHERS

Once we understand who we are to God and have accepted, no matter what mistakes we've made or who we were before knowing Christ as Lord, that we can minister to other women, we should *mentor* our sisters—especially young girls in their formative years. The incredible truth that "I am valuable and important to God" must be shared from one generation to the next.

When you fall in love with God, it is natural to love on your sisters. As Matthew 22:37-39 tells you, "Jesus said unto him, Thou shalt love the Lord thy God with all thy heart, and with all thy soul, and with all thy mind. This is the first and great commandment. And the second is like unto it, Thou shalt love thy neighbor as thyself." Loving the Lord gives you the ability to love yourself and others. God's love will flow through you, and as women of substance, we must display this love toward one another. As we walk together in unity, accepting each other for who we are, then your interactions with your sister in Christ will help her share the same love with others and to become more like Him.

When you fall in love with God, it is natural to love on your sisters.

Mentoring is how one person guides another along their spiritual path and life journey toward maturity in God. Mentoring other sisters through the good and the bad and exhibiting God's love through obedience is a command from the Lord. The best mentors are those who have allowed other women of God to mentor them first.

183

How do you grow your substance in others by mentoring them? First, seek out a female within your own family, church, or community, and make time in your schedule to mentor her. Feel free to start by going out for a cup of coffee, making a nice lunch for the two of you at your home, or taking a walk in the park together. Second, be honest, patient, loving, and nonjudgmental with her. This must come from a loving heart filled with the unconditional "agape" love that only comes from God. Share your testimony all along the way, knowing that your story (like mine shared throughout this book) will be very powerful and effective because it will show your sister that you were not always the woman she sees today.

Finally, establish a trusting relationship where your sister can share her innermost secrets with you and feel safe doing so. Keep in mind this directive from Galatians 6:1-2. "Brethren, if a man be overtaken in a fault, ye which are spiritual, restore such an one in the spirit of meekness; considering thyself, lest thou also be tempted. Bear ye one another's burdens, and so fulfil the law of Christ." Show empathy toward your sister, and if she makes a mistake or falls into sin, be loving enough to restore her to yourself and to your God. Be willing to listen, listen—and listen again. Listening before giving advice gives you a chance to hear from her heart so that God can reveal to you what to pray about and how to respond. Don't be in a hurry to give an answer. It is more important to provide time for her to make the transformation herself so God can heal the hurt within her as He works in her life.

Here are 10 keys to being a successful spiritual mentor to your sister.

1. Be accepting. No matter how she believes or lives and regardless of her issues, you must lovingly accept her faults. Remember, someone once did the same for you.

2. Be available. You must show up and be fully present when needed. You cannot mentor someone you never see.

3. Be sincere. God has placed you in that person's life, so be honest about your feelings toward her. Be free from pretense or deceit out of genuine commitment to her and to God.

4. Never give up on her. No matter how often she falls or how disappointing her choices, remember that there *will* be a change in her life. As long as God has not released you from mentoring that individual, keep seeing her as a new person in Christ Jesus. Do this in prayer if, for whatever reason, you cannot be there for her in person right away.

5. Be patient. This will help you to never give up. Remember you are bearing with another person (Romans 12:10), and this is only done through the strength of the Lord.

6. Be open. See her and her issues through God's perspective and not your own—for many times, we can establish our own righteousness. We tend to pick and choose what sins we are going to avoid and place more judgment upon others as a result. Yet if you keep a closed mind and avoid what or who is or is not more sinful, how can you be an effective witness and exhibit the righteous things of God? Trust in the Holy Spirit to help you correctly address that which may be contrary to the Word of God in the most effective and, at times, unconventional way. You'll recall from Chapter 5 how my mother, Vernell, invited a prostitute to come to our house for food and to rest and talk. That was considered unconventional, yet my mother never made a differentiation between her and women who were in the church. My mother never judged her. She loved her with the love of Christ and led her to Jesus.

7. Be compassionate. Compassion—the sympathetic pity and concern for the sufferings or misfortunes of your sister—goes hand in hand with love.

8. **Be discreet.** Always maintain confidentiality without exception.

9. **LIVE THE LIFE YOU ARE GUIDING OTHERS TO LIVE.** I capitalized this one because there is no such thing as an effective hypocrite. Remember the saying, "Don't do what I do, but do as I say?" This will not work! My mother use to say, "The best witness is a living witness." Be an example of the Word of God in all that you say and do.

10. **Possess the fruit of the Spirit:** love, joy, peace, long-suffering, gentleness, goodness, faith, meekness, and temperance (Galatians 5:22-23). These characteristics of the Holy Spirit are the evidence of our new spiritual birth through faith in Jesus Christ. When you give to others what God has given to you, you will *truly* live out your substance.

Daughter of the King, thank you for joining me on this journey through the Word of God, beginning in Genesis and continuing throughout its pages. We've met some amazing women of Scripture, and I've shared bits of my story along the way. It is my fervent desire, as I use the content shared in this book to teach and speak, that you will come into your destiny and thrive as a woman of God. Remember, you are designed with incredible substance to achieve incredible things for the Lord!

Sources

1 https://www.usgs.gov/special-topic/water-science-school/science
   /water-you-water-and-human-body?qt-science_center_objects=0#qt
   -science_center_objects
2 https://www.medicalnewstoday.com/articles/325174#:~:text=As%
   20a%20general%20rule%20of,age

Made in the USA
Monee, IL
23 October 2021

46ea7ed4-9649-4698-a9aa-b5a1606f01aeR01